CONSEQUENCES

Stories about Personal Safety for Assembly and P.S.H.E.

Gordon Aspland

SOUTHGATE

First published 2003 by Southgate Publishers Ltd

Southgate Publishers Ltd
The Square, Sandford, Crediton, Devon EX17 4LW

Printed and bound in Great Britain by Short Run Press Ltd, Exeter, Devon.

British Library Cataloguing in Publication Data
A CIP catalogue record for this book is available from the British Library.

ISBN 1–85741–155–2

CONTENTS

Introduction

My previous assembly books each covered a range of issues affecting children. *Consequences* is different in that the stories specifically look at the dangers children could encounter in the world around them. Another feature is that these stories are aimed particularly at Years 5 and 6; if you wish to use them with younger children it is recommended that you read them first to see how appropriate they will be in your context.

The stories address three types of danger that could affect children's personal safety:

- dangers arising from accidental situations, sometimes caused by the results of inappropriate behaviour (as in stories 3, 4, 8, 9, 12 and 13);
- situations caused by children deliberately putting themselves at risk (as in stories 1, 6, 10, 11, 14 and 15);
- situations where children are targeted by others for some kind of abuse (as in stories 2, 5 and 7).

Is there a need for stories that cover these issues? You only need to look at the statistics published by RoSPA to see how relevant the matter of personal safety is. Their statistics make horrendous reading. Here are just a few of them:

- In 2001, the figures for children under the age of fifteen show that 107 pedestrians were killed, 25 cyclists were killed and a total of 3686 were seriously hurt.
- In 2000, other deaths for under-fifteens included 10 from poisoning, 17 from falls, 38 from fire, 94 from drowning and 50 from homicide.
- In 1999, children who required hospital treatment included 1,008,239 from falls, 643,135 struck by object/person, and 34,587 from poisoning.
- There is a big increase in numbers from eleven-year-olds to twelve-year-olds (the change from primary to secondary) because when children go to secondary school this tends to be without parent supervision and they also

demand more personal freedom as they copy older children.

Most accidents happen: between late afternoon and early evening; in the summer; during school holidays and at the weekends.

The RoSPA website (www.rospa.co.uk) is full of useful statistics that could be discussed in the classroom.

The title of the book, *Consequences*, was chosen to demonstrate that children are generally unaware of the many new situations that they can encounter in their daily lives. They have limited perception of potential dangers because of their lack of experience. They are also naturally inquisitive and have a high spirit of adventure. Boys in particular are prone to showing off, especially among friends.

I have written these stories in order to help teachers address the issues of personal danger with the children in their care. I have tried to provide a variety of settings to stimulate discussion about the various risks that are encountered in these stories.

Please note, stories 1, 9 and 11 end with children either being killed or being seriously hurt. I was uncertain about whether to include endings like this, but when I trialled the stories with Year 6 classes they were unanimous that this gave the stories more credibility.

Gordon Aspland
2003

CONSEQUENCES

1
The Storm

THEME: the dangers of playing by rough seas

He could feel the waves pulling him under, sucking the breath from his body. He was being bashed against the rocks, but that wasn't what was really hurting him – it was the pain in his lungs that seared through his body.

What is happening to this boy? How do you think he got himself into this predicament?

Here is the whole story.

The doorbell rang and Tom rushed to the door. It was Leroy, his best mate from school.

"Is David with you?" asked Tom.

"He said he'll meet us down there," replied Leroy.

Tom grabbed his skateboard and shouted out to his mother, "I'm off now, Mum!"

His mother appeared by the kitchen door, soap suds dripping from her hands. "Thanks for helping me with the dishes," she said sarcastically. "Where are you going?"

"Just down to the seafront with our skateboards. I'll only be gone a couple of hours. Leave the dishes, I'll dry them when I get back." Tom knew that his promise was really a false one, his mother would finish them off – she always did.

They lived in a small town by the seaside and the local children enjoyed congregating by the quay next to the harbour. There was a large concrete area where they played on their skateboards, much to the annoyance of the older adults. It was an unusually warm, still evening when Tom and Leroy met up with David and his younger brother, Ben. The brothers were just lounging about drinking cans of coke.

As Tom and Leroy arrived at the front the evening lights went on, illuminating the whole quayside. The boys started to play on their skateboards, zig-zagging around the dustbins, jumping and flipping the skateboards between their feet. But the evening air was very heavy, too stuffy for energetic activities so they soon

7

stopped and sat down on the edge of the quay, feet dangling over the water.

"Are you going to watch the rugby match tomorrow?" asked David.

"What match?" asked Leroy.

"England against Wales," replied Ben.

" The match of the season when Wales will trounce England," declared David.

Then Tom, followed by Leroy, started calling out "England, England". This annoyed David and Ben, who were from Wales, so they started chanting "Wales, Wales". The boys jumped on their skateboards and started racing about, still chanting. David stopped by the lifebuoy for a rest. He noticed that it was a torpedo lifebuoy and thought how similar it looked to a rugby ball. Looking carefully around to make sure no one was about, he got out his penknife and cut the rope attached to the lifebuoy.

"Ben, catch!" he shouted and threw the lifebuoy to his brother, pretending it was a rugby ball. Tom and Leroy joined in and soon it was two against two, England versus Wales! Tom managed to intercept a pass between Ben and David. David chased after him and instead of trying to throw the lifebuoy to Ben he just threw it behind him in any old direction. The four boys stopped and watched as their rugby ball bounced and then rolled to the edge of the quay.

"Quick, get it!" shouted David. Ben was closest but he was too late and they watched in disappointment as the lifebuoy rolled over the edge and into the sea. Before they could even think about retrieving it they heard a shout .

"What do you think you're doing, you little vandals?" shouted a man who had just walked out of a nearby pub and saw them playing with the lifebuoy. They didn't wait to explain but grabbed their skateboards and ran away. It wasn't until the illuminated quay was well behind them that they stopped to get their breath back.

"Do you think he knew us?" asked Tom, worried about what his mother might say.

"Nah," said David, "it was too dark. Are you coming round to our house to watch the match?" he asked Tom and Leroy. Both boys said they would and, with that, they all went off to their own homes. Meanwhile, the tide was going out and with it the lifebuoy disappeared out to sea.

What could be the consequences of the lifebuoy going missing?

That night the weather broke. First the wind came, then the rain. People woke in the morning to a ferocious storm and just as they thought it couldn't get any worse, it did. The wind got stronger and it became one of the worst storms for years. People were warned not to make any unnecessary journeys and especially to stay away from the coast, where the waves at high tide were crashing over the sea defences.

The four boys met at David and Ben's home to watch the rugby but they were disappointed when the game was cancelled because of the weather.

"What shall we do now?" asked a bored Leroy.

"Let's take our skateboards down to the quay," suggested David.

"It's too wet for skateboarding," said Tom.

"We could look at the waves," proposed Ben.

"Would your parents let you go?" asked Tom.

"They're both at work," said David. "They haven't said we can't go down there."

"Have your parents said you can't go down to the quay?" asked David.

"No," said Leroy.

"No," agreed Tom, "but my mum thought I was coming here to watch the rugby."

"Oh, come on!" urged David. "We're only going to look."

So the boys put on their jackets and braved the rough weather to go down to the quay to watch the waves. It was a spectacular sight, with the waves hitting the harbour wall and shooting water and spray high up into the air. There were quite a few people there to see it, though most were watching from a distance because they didn't want to get wet.

"Look!" shouted David as he pointed to some older boys running in front of the waves. When a wave dashed itself against the quay wall the boys would run under the mountain of water that rose into the air and then run out before the water tumbled down on to the quay, avoiding getting too wet. "That looks wicked. Come on!" he shouted to the others.

Leroy and Tom stood back while David led Ben on to the quay. A mountain of water rose into the air and the two brothers joined the older boys as they ran underneath it then out before the water cascaded down. They came running up to Tom and Leroy. "Come on!" called Ben. "It's really cool!"

Leroy finally couldn't resist and he followed them as they ran under the waves again. Leroy was a bit slow and got rather wet but he was laughing when they ran back to Tom.

"Why don't you try it?" asked Leroy.

"Come on, Tom. Are you scared?" taunted David.

The three boys ran back to the waves again. Tom stepped forward to run after them – he wasn't going to have David call him scared. He caught up with them just as another wave came crashing over. He turned to run out before it came tumbling down when he saw Ben slip on the wet concrete. Tom, Leroy and David managed to escape the crashing wall of water, but when the water pulled back there was no sign of Ben.

Ben had felt his feet shoot out from under him and then instantly he was engulfed by a wall of water. When the wave smashed down on him he felt as though there were hundreds of heavy hands grabbing him and pulling him into the sea. There was a moment when he was suspended in the air and then he was submerged in the open water. He could feel the waves pulling him under, sucking the breath from his body. He was being bashed against the rocks, but that wasn't what was really hurting him – it was the pain in his lungs that seared through his body.

On the quay David was rooted to the spot, sickened by what he was seeing. He saw his brother pop to the surface with one arm raised, desperately waving for help. Two or three adults came rushing over. One looked at the case where the lifebuoy should have been but found it had gone. Another large wave engulfed

Ben and then he disappeared. Tom and Leroy looked at each other, then they looked at David – it was like being in a nightmare.

One of the adults used a mobile phone to call the emergency services. Very soon the boys could see the lifeboat being launched. But would it be in time?

Discussion:

1. What were the consequences of David taking the lifebuoy? How was he feeling about this now?
2. It was David who took the lifebuoy. Was he the only one to blame? What could the others have done?
3. Why did the boys play under the crashing waves?
4. What are the lessons to be learnt from this story?

(Discussion should include: respecting the sea; vandalising safety equipment; copying other people who are doing something reckless; resisting peer pressure when you know what is suggested is wrong; being sensitive to the feelings of others.)

2
Can I Help you?

THEME: physical abuse from someone known

She could hear his running footsteps behind her, getting closer and closer. Brambles tugged at her clothes and branches whipped across her face as she struggled to race away. She could hear his heavy breathing and swearing as the branches hit his face. "Come back!" he shouted. "I won't hurt you!" Roots of a tree seemed to grab her feet and she found herself falling …

What is happening here? Where do you think it is taking place? How do you think the girl has got herself into this situation?

Here is the whole story.

Yasmin, Julie and Rachel were very close friends. They started playschool together and were in the same class right through primary school. Yasmin was a musician, she could play three instruments and was always going to lessons on a Saturday morning. So the routine most Saturdays was that Julie would go to Rachel's house in the morning and then they would go into town and meet Yasmin at the café after she had finished her lessons. It was only in the last few months that they had been allowed to do this and it made them feel very grown up. Rachel's mum worked in the clothes shop opposite the café so they always reported to her when they arrived.

Julie and Rachel stood outside the café waiting for Yasmin. Rachel's mum said they could wait in the shop but they didn't want to be seen in a clothes shop for older ladies. "Where is she?" asked Rachel impatiently, looking at her watch. "She's usually here by now."

"We could go into the café now and wait for her there," suggested Julie.

"Have you forgotten, I've got to buy a CD for my brother's birthday? Maybe we could go in later if we have time," said Rachel.

"Sometimes her teacher asks her to stay back for some extra help," Julie tried to explain. The two girls waited another five minutes but there was still no sign of

Yasmin. "Look, why don't we tell your mum we're going to the CD shop? Yasmin's bound to pop in there when she doesn't see us in the café," suggested Julie.

So they told Rachel's mum where they were going and went off to the other end of town to the CD shop. Meanwhile, Yasmin was dashing to the café from the other direction. Julie was right, she had been kept late by the clarinet teacher and she had to do some fruit and veg shopping for her mum. So she arrived at the café, carrying bags of fresh food, a bag of music and a case containing her clarinet, only to find that the other two had gone. She went over to the clothes shop and looked into the window. The girls weren't there and Rachel's mum was busy with a customer so she didn't go in. She was really annoyed, especially as she was hoping that the other two would help her carry some of her things home.

Yasmin decided to go home alone. She lived about a mile away, too close for a bus but a hard walk when you were carrying lots of bags! There was a short cut through a park but her mum told her she mustn't use that route if she was alone. Her hands were hurting from carrying the bags. She stopped at the entrance to the park and looked in. There were people in the park walking their dogs – it seemed very peaceful.

"Hello, Yasmin," said a voice behind her. "You seem loaded down."

Yasmin jumped, she hadn't heard anybody coming up behind her. She whirled around and saw it was Mike, her family's next-door neighbour. He and his wife had moved in about a year ago. They had two small boys who Yasmin adored. Mike and his wife often allowed Yasmin to come over and help look after them. Mike was unemployed and looked after the boys when his wife went out to work at Sainsbury's. He was the one who asked Yasmin if she wanted to come over and help with the boys. Sometimes he would sit and watch her and say nice things about her hair or the clothes she wore. It usually made her feel good, though the last time he had said that, he'd stroked her hair and that made her feel awkward. Since then she hadn't been in to visit the boys.

"Hello, Mr Bedow," Yasmin said.

"Oh, come on now, you should be calling me Mike. We haven't seen you for a while. Is everything all right?"

"Yes, I've been busy with school work and I've got a clarinet exam soon so I've been busy practising," explained Yasmin.

"I've heard you practising – you're very good. You should come over and play for the boys, they would like that."

Yasmin stood there awkwardly, not knowing what to say. The bags were getting heavy and she needed to get home.

"Here, let me take that heavy bag for you, I'm on my way home as well," said Mike.

"Thank you," was all Yasmin could say.

Mike began to walk through the park gate but Yasmin hesitated.

What should Yasmin do? After all, Mike is trying to help her.

"Come on, this is a much quicker way home," encouraged Mike. "Surely you weren't going the long way home?"

"Yes, but Mum said I shouldn't go through the park on my own, you know, in case of strangers."

"Well, you're not on your own and I'm not a stranger, so come on." With that, Mike strode into the park with Yasmin following behind him. The dog walkers had disappeared down another path so there was no one about as they walked into the park. When they were out of sight of the road Mike stopped. "I nearly forgot, I promised the boys some conkers, that was why I was out here. Would you help me get some?"

"I don't know. I've really got to get home," said Yasmin.

"With me helping you, you'll be home in no time, so come on. You can help me, just this once?" coaxed Mike.

Without waiting for her reply he set off away from the lane and up a winding little path through the trees and bracken. Yasmin followed. She had never been up this path before, she didn't know where it was going. She stayed close to Mike because she didn't want to get lost.

"There it is," said Mike, "the best horse chestnut tree in the area and hardly any kids know about it. Look at all those conkers on the ground. Come on, help me pick some of them up."

It was a huge tree, right in the middle of the wood. Mike put the shopping bag down and took out a plastic bag from his pocket. He began to put conkers into the bag, so Yasmin put her things down to do the same. She picked up a handful of conkers and took them over to Mike. She put them into his bag and then turned away to look for more. Suddenly his arms were around her, gripping her tightly. He started speaking, telling her to be nice to him and she knew then she was in real danger. She remembered being told at school about what to do if an adult grabbed you from behind. She screamed as loud as she could. Mike put his hand over her mouth so hard she could hardly breathe. But that was what she expected him to do – now she was able to bite on his hand. She bit down so hard she could feel her teeth sinking into his flesh. He took his hand away, shouting, and then she was only held by one arm. She raised her right leg and kicked back against his leg, scraping her hard heel against his shin. He threw her to the ground in anger but instead of lying there, cowering, she got to her feet and ran away as fast as she could, just escaping his clutching arms.

She had caught him off guard, he wasn't expecting her to fight back the way she did. But he was now very angry and started to run after her. She could hear his running footsteps behind her, getting closer and closer. Brambles tugged at her clothes and branches whipped across her face as she struggled to race away. She could hear his heavy breathing and swearing as the branches hit his face. "Come back!" he shouted, "I won't hurt you!" Roots of a tree seemed to grab her feet and she found herself falling. She went head first down a little slope and suddenly she rolled out on to the main lane leading through the park.

"Goodness! Where did you come from?" said an elderly man, staring down at her.

"I told you I heard screams, Bert. Are you in trouble?" asked his wife. Bert and

Mavis were out walking their dogs and were quite shocked to see the state Yasmin was in. They knelt down and helped Yasmin to her feet. Yasmin looked wildly behind her to see if Mike was still there but there was no sign of him. Shock suddenly hit her and she started to cry uncontrollably. Mavis took her into her arms and tried to comfort her, while Bert took out his mobile phone to call the police.

Discussion:

1. What should Yasmin tell the police?
2. At what point did Yasmin make the wrong decision?
3. What were the consequences of her friends not waiting for her?
4. What signs can you look out for that tell you an adult could be harmful to you?

(Discussion should include: when an adult asks you to keep a secret, maybe about gifts or having a cuddle; being too familiar or staring at you; inviting you to their house or out for treats on your own; being especially complimentary.)

3
The Broken Vase

CONSEQUENCES

THEME: how losing your temper can affect others

She could feel the broken shards of glass pierce her body. She cried in pain as she tried to walk, leaving drips of blood across the floor.

What do you think has happened? How do you think the glass got on to the floor?

Here is the whole story.

"Will you hurry up!" shouted Mark as he banged on the bathroom door.

Claire, his fifteen-year-old sister, opened the door and stood glowering at him. She had a large bath towel around her body and a smaller towel wrapped around her hair. Steam billowed out from behind her. "Keep your hair on!" was all she said as she went to her bedroom and slammed the door shut. Mark dashed into the bathroom. He was in a hurry to get ready as he was meeting Tom and Leroy at the park for a game of football. He wanted to make sure he was in Tom's team because Tom was a brilliant footballer and he never lost.

Mark finished washing and raced downstairs for breakfast. His mum was getting bowls of cereal and cups of coffee ready. But before he could start, his mother told him, "Wait, Dad had to go into the office early this morning so before you eat could you sort the dog out?"

"Why can't you do it?"

"What, like this?" she said putting her arms out to show she was still in her dressing gown. "If you haven't got time to take her up the road at least take her around the back and play ball with her and make sure she does her jobs." Sascha stood there wagging her tail; she didn't mind who took her as long as she went out. She was half Jack Russell and half border collie and she liked nothing better than chasing after a ball in the garden or going for long walks.

Mark grabbed a tennis ball and went outside, with Sascha leaping up and down with excitement. "Go on, do your jobs first," he shouted, pointing to the grass. Sascha knew the routine – she dashed on to the grass, performed and then ran back to him, waiting for the ball to be thrown. Mark threw it and Sascha dashed after it as if she were chasing a rat and then trotted back and dropped the ball at Mark's feet for him to throw again. They did this three times and then Mark ran back into the house, followed by a disappointed dog.

"That was quick," remarked his mother. "Here's your cereal."

Claire was sitting at the table, dressed but with her hair still in a towel. She was painting her nails a bright red. "Does she have to do that at the table?" demanded Mark.

"I'm not doing you any harm," pouted Claire as she continued.

"That stuff smells!" he said between mouthfuls of cereal.

"Don't gobble your food like that," his mother told him.

"I'm in a hurry, the practice starts in …" he looked at his watch, "fifteen minutes and it takes at least ten to cycle to the park."

"Then you'll be five minutes early," declared Claire, as she rose from the table to go back to her room and start drying her hair.

"Dishes, Claire," reminded her mother.

"I can't, I've just done my nails," she argued. "Why can't he do them?" She pointed a long finger with a newly painted red nail in Mark's direction.

"No way! It's not my turn and I've got to get to the park," said Mark as he leapt to his feet, gulped the last of his coffee and dashed out of the house with his football bag over his shoulder.

Mum threw a tea towel at Claire. "I'll wash, you dry."

For both Mark and Claire the morning went from good to bad and then worse. Mark got to the park just in time as the other boys started to pick teams and he was delighted to be with his best friends, Tom and Leroy. The game started well for them and they were soon two goals up, with Tom having scored both. Then two older boys joined in. One of them was the brother of a boy in the other team so the two joined that side and soon Mark's team was losing heavily.

One of the older boys was running with the ball towards Mark. Mark was getting really fed up, the two big boys were not invited to play but he couldn't do anything about it. As the big boy came towards him Mark did something very reckless, he slid into the tackle with both feet, won the ball but also sent the big boy sprawling on to the ground. Mark put his hand up to say sorry for tripping him. He thought they would just continue the game but the big boy came up to him and without saying anything punched him in the face. Mark fell over, stunned, as the big boy towered over him, shaking his fist and saying, "Don't do that again!"

The game went on but Mark didn't have any heart for it. He was relieved when lunchtime came and they all had to go home. The side of his face was sore but Tom said it only looked a little bit red. He would tell his parents that somebody whacked the ball hard and it hit him in the face. He was looking forward to the afternoon when he could watch sport on TV.

Meanwhile, Claire was looking forward to meeting her boyfriend, Paul, in town. With her hair now dry and carefully brushed, and dressed in her favourite jeans and top she patiently waited outside the big department store. He wanted her to help him buy a birthday present for his mum. She waited for fifteen minutes then her mobile phone rang. It was Paul – he couldn't make it that morning, he said. A mate of his had got some tickets for the Leyton Orient match away to Bristol so it meant leaving that morning to get to Bristol. Claire was furious. All that time getting ready, catching a bus into town, waiting, and for what? She turned her mobile off while Paul was still explaining and stomped back to the bus station. She had some good films on tape; she would go home and after lunch she would spend the afternoon watching one of them.

Both Mark and Claire have a TV in their bedroom but only the set in the lounge has a video machine and only that one has Sky sports. What is going to happen that afternoon?

Claire was sitting in the lounge, looking at her tapes and eating a sandwich when Mark came in. "What's happened to your face?" she asked him.

"A football hit me. Where's everyone?"

"Dad sorted out his problem in the office so he came home. He's taken Sascha out for a long walk and Mum is visiting Gran," explained Claire.

Mark made himself a sandwich, took it into the lounge, grabbed the remote control and turned on the TV to watch football.

"Oh no you don't!" announced Claire. "I'm watching a film, you can watch football in your room." She grabbed the remote control from his hand and switched the TV programme to the video channel.

"Hey, I was watching that!" shouted Mark. "And for your information I can't watch the Man U match because it's on Sky and I don't have Sky upstairs." With that, he snatched the remote control back. Claire was furious: she wasn't going to miss out on seeing a film because of a football match. They started to struggle for the remote control and Claire hit out at Mark in a fit of temper. She hit his sore face and he cried out in pain. He stood up and was so angry he threw the remote control at Claire. She ducked and both of them watched as the remote control flew through the air and collided with Mum's favourite crystal vase. They were stunned as they watched the vase, first slowly and then picking up speed, topple to the floor. The crystal vase hit the wooden floor and smashed into thousands of pieces.

"Look what you've done!" screamed Claire.

"You made me do it!" Mark screamed back.

Just then the front door opened and Dad came in from his walk with Sascha. He let her off the lead and she came bounding into the lounge, tail wagging, to say hello to them. Before either Claire or Mark could stop her, Sascha was stepping and falling on the pieces of smashed vase. She could feel the broken shards of glass pierce her body. She cried in pain as she tried to walk, leaving drips of blood across the floor.

"What on earth has gone on here?" shouted Dad. He quickly picked Sascha up and carried her into the kitchen, with Mark and Claire following. He placed her on her back and told the children to hold her down while he examined her paws and lower body.

"This is no good, we'll have to take her to the vet right away," he said. Sascha lay very still, too shocked from the pain to move. "You two will have to hold her in the car while I drive," he told them. "And you can explain how this happened on the way!"

Sascha survived; she hadn't cut any major arteries. She was very uncomfortable for a few weeks, but not as uncomfortable as Claire and Mark felt every time they looked at her.

Discussion:
1. Whose fault do you think the accident is?
2. Why were both Mark and Claire in such a bad mood when they got home?
3. How could they have resolved the problem without losing their tempers?

(Explore how conflicts are resolved at home and how compromises are reached.)

4
The Lemonade Bottle

> **THEME: the dangers of storing harmful liquids in drinks bottles**

"My eyes, my eyes! I can't see!" The liquid was everywhere. The pain it caused was excruciating.

What do you think has happened? What kind of liquid could it be?

Here is the whole story.

Julie's mum was in a hurry. Julie was having some friends round for tea and afterwards they were going to watch the Eurovision Song contest. Her mum had promised to buy some pizzas and lemonade, but her car had broken down and by the time the rescue service came out to fix it she had very little time left to shop, get home and put the pizzas in the oven before Julie's friends arrived.

Mum raced into the house and put the shopping down on a kitchen counter. But she wasn't very careful and the bag toppled over. A bottle of bleach, a strong cleaner, fell out and she could only watch as it fell off the counter on to the floor.

"Oh no!" she cried. She picked up the bleach and quickly put it into the sink because it was leaking – the bottle must have cracked when it landed on the floor. She frantically looked around for another container to pour the bleach into. She looked under the sink and in other cupboards but she couldn't find anything. She then opened the fridge and saw a nearly empty lemonade bottle. She took it out and emptied the last dregs of the lemonade down the drain, rinsed the bottle and then poured the bleach into it.

Why is this a very stupid thing to do?

Julie's mum screwed the top tightly on to the lemonade bottle. Just at that moment the telephone rang. She put the empty bleach bottle into the bin and went to answer the phone, leaving the lemonade bottle on the counter. It was Rachel's mother asking if it would be all right for Rachel to stay the night as she and her husband were going to the cinema that evening.

While the two mothers chatted, Julie was up in her bedroom getting ready for the evening. After putting the finishing touches to the small amount of make-up she was allowed to wear, she wandered downstairs and into the kitchen. She saw the lemonade bottle and was just about to pour herself a drink when she realised that the liquid was warm. She hated warm lemonade. She put the bottle in the fridge and then went into the lounge to put the TV on. Her friends should be arriving soon.

"I've got a surprise for you," said her mother as she came into the lounge. "That was Rachel's mum on the phone asking if Rachel could stay the night."

"Oh, yes please," shouted Julie with excitement.

"Don't worry, I said yes." Her mum looked at her watch. "Good heavens! They'll be here soon. I must put the pizzas in the oven. How many did you say are coming over?"

"Five altogether, including me. There's Rachel and Yasmin, Tom and Leroy."

"Two boys, eh? I'll have to watch you lot!"

"Mum! They're only friends!" said Julie, though she did have a soft spot for Tom and she was hoping he would sit next to her during the evening.

Her mother went back to the kitchen to put her shopping away and turn the oven on ready for the pizzas. She had also bought bottles of lemonade and cola and two flavours of crisps.

The doorbell rang and when Julie answered it she found Yasmin and Rachel there. They went upstairs, giggling and chatting about the song contest. As Julie showed Rachel where she was going to sleep she heard the doorbell ring again. Her mum got to the door before her and showed Tom and Leroy into the lounge.

"Thanks, Mum," said Julie, giving her that you-can-now-leave-the-room look.

"That's OK, Julie. So I won't disturb you again maybe you can come and get the crisps while I check the pizzas."

The boys sat down on the sofa and Julie went out to get the crisps. When she came back she found Rachel and Yasmin also sitting on the sofa, with Yasmin next to Tom! This really annoyed Julie, but all she could do was put the crisps down and sit on the single chair.

Yasmin was really pleased: she'd been hoping to sit next to Tom. She was a bit put out that Julie had not invited her to stay the night, along with Rachel. She was aware of Julie glowering at her for taking the seat next to Tom and this made her even happier.

Julie's mum popped her head round the door. "The pizzas are nearly ready. Are you going to offer your guests a drink?"

Julie got up and asked, rather unenthusiastically, "What would you like. We've got lemonade and coke."

"I'll have coke, please," said Leroy.

"Same for me," said Tom.

"And me," said Rachel.

"I'll have lemonade," said Yasmin.

You would be different, thought Julie as she went into the kitchen to get the drinks. First she poured out the glasses of coke, including one for herself. She was about to open a new bottle of lemonade when she remembered the bottle in the fridge. She got it out and noticed that there was no fizz when she opened it. Good, she thought, nice and flat.

When she went back to the lounge she turned rigid with fury. Yasmin had put her hand on top of Tom's. Even though Tom was looking decidedly uncomfortable, Yasmin was glowing. Julie couldn't bear it – Yasmin was deliberately ruining her evening. She put the drinks down and picked up the glass of lemonade. As she was just about to give Yasmin the drink she pretended to trip and threw the glass of liquid over Yasmin. But her aim wasn't very good. Though some of the liquid went on to Yasmin's jumper, the rest splashed into Tom's face.

He instantly jumped up, clutching at his face, screaming, "My eyes, my eyes! I can't see!" The liquid was everywhere. The pain it caused was excruciating.
Julie's mother came running in. "What's happening?" she cried.

Tom continued to scream in pain and was madly rubbing at his eyes.

"It's only lemonade!" shouted Julie.

Her mother reached Tom and stopped him from rubbing his eyes. She instantly knew what the liquid was – she could smell that it was bleach. She pulled Tom into the kitchen and immediately turned the cold water tap on. Then she grabbed a jug, filled it with water, pushed Tom's head over the sink and poured water over his face and eyes. "How did you manage to throw bleach at him?" she demanded.

"I don't understand. I thought it was lemonade!" replied Julie, pointing at the bottle of lemonade.

Her mother knew then what had happened and with a dreadful feeling she knew it was her fault. "Oh my God! Don't touch that lemonade bottle. Julie, I want you to telephone the ambulance, so dial 999." She continued to fill the jug and pour water over Tom's face. The cooling water was having an effect. Tom stopped shrieking and let her pull his eyes open to pour more water over them.

Then Yasmin began to scream. She was standing in the kitchen, looking at her hands. She had tried to brush the liquid off her jumper and now the bleach was beginning to burn her hands.

"Leroy, Rachel! Take her to the downstairs toilet and run the cold water over her hands. Hurry!" said Julie's mum.

As well as phoning for an ambulance Julie also phoned Tom's parents and they arrived about the same time as the ambulance. Her mother gave the paramedics the empty bottle of bleach so that they would know exactly what had caused the burning and how to treat it. Yasmin's mother arrived and took Yasmin by car to the same casualty department.

When they had gone, Julie's mum sank into a chair.

"You were great, Mum," said Julie. "How did you know what to do?"

"I've just finished a first aid course at work," her mum replied. "But it's a shame they didn't teach me some common sense as well." She then buried her face in her hands as she realised just how foolish she had been.

Tom stayed in hospital for a few days. He was lucky – because Julie's mother was quick in splashing him with water there was no permanent damage to his eyes. Yasmin's hands also made a full recovery.

Discussion:

1. What did Julie's mum mean when she said, "it's a shame they didn't teach me some common sense'?
2. How did jealousy play a part in this story?
3. What would have happened if one of the group had drunk the bleach?

(Discuss how you would treat somebody who drank a chemical like bleach.)

5
The Chase

THEME: how jealousy can make us do dangerous things

Suddenly another boy was right in front of him. He slammed on the brakes but he was too late. There was a sickening thud and the boy flew on to the bonnet and crashed into the windscreen before sliding back down to the road. The driver quickly got out, afraid of what he was going to see ...

What has happened? How do you think this boy found himself in front of the car? How was the driver feeling?

Here is the whole story.

Tom and Leroy were members of a gang. It was a small gang, just a group of lads getting together to play football or hanging about in the park, play-fighting and making secret dens. Mark was the recognised leader; he was the one who decided what they were going to do. Once Tom had argued about how teams were organised for a game of football. Mark had just thumped him in the stomach – there was no argument after that.

The gang didn't get into too much mischief. The worst thing they did was to sneak into gardens in the autumn and steal apples so they could have a feast in their den. Only once did they get really into trouble with the Community Police Officer. Mark had led a raid on an allotment where they stole pocketfuls of small, cherry-like tomatoes. Mark had this silly idea about dropping them on to cars as they drove under the footbridge. Most of the time they missed but one motorist who had a tomato splattered on her windscreen used her mobile phone to call the police. The boys were so intent on what they were doing they didn't see the police officer walking up behind them. He was very cross and told them that they could easily cause an accident. He wrote down all their names and addresses and all their parents were informed about what they had been doing. Tom and Leroy were both banned by their parents from going down to the park for two weeks.

Some months later Tom and Leroy met up with the others at the park. It was a warm summer evening and they were having a half-hearted game of football. They soon got tired and sat on the swings. They were really too big for the swings but as there were no adults about with toddlers they took them over.

"What do you think about the new boy?" asked Tom. At the beginning of the week a new boy had joined their class, his name was Charles but he wanted everybody to call him Charlie. He seemed to settle very quickly into his new school and was soon accepted by the other boys.

"He's OK," said David. "He's good at football."

"He's got a cracking left foot," agreed Leroy.

"He's a bit of a know-all," said Mark. "He's always putting his hand up with the answer."

"Yeh, Miss kept saying 'Well done, Charlie! Are you the only one awake today?" said Tom in a pretend teacher voice. The other boys laughed.

"He's not that good at football," said Mark.

"He scored two goals against you at lunchtime today," replied Leroy.

"He was lucky. Come on, let's finish our game," muttered Mark. The truth was he had taken an instant dislike to Charlie. Mark was the boss in the playground, he organised the football game and he always made sure that players like Tom and Leroy were on his side. They usually won, but over the last few days they had lost a couple of games and the main difference was Charlie playing for the other team. This made Mark angry; he wasn't a good loser. Today he asked if Charlie would like to play in his team but Charlie said no, that wouldn't be fair sides. This made Charlie even more popular with some of the other boys.

On the way home Tom and Leroy discussed the problem of Mark and Charlie.

"I think there is going to be trouble between them. Mark doesn't like losing," said Tom.

"He can be real nutcase sometimes," agreed Leroy.

"Charlie's all right. I like him," said Tom.

The next day was Friday and at lunchtime the boys were about to play football when it started to pour with rain and they had to go in. Mark was annoyed, he wanted to get his own back on Charlie for beating him the day before. He wandered about the classroom and picked up Julie's eraser. Julie was just finishing off some work and needed to use the eraser.

"Give that back!" shouted Julie.

"Come and get it!" called Mark.

Julie stood up and held out her hand. "Come on, Mark, give it back," she demanded.

Mark threw the eraser to Leroy, who then threw it to Tom. But Tom liked Julie so he accidentally-on-purpose dropped it on the floor and Julie ran to pick it up. "Butterfingers," mocked Mark. Mark continued to prowl around the room. He noticed Charlie reading a book. "What are you reading?" he asked.

"The Hobbit," Charlie replied. "It's really good. Have you read it?"

"Nah, don't like reading." Then Mark noticed Charlie's football under his chair. He picked it up and began to bounce it and throw it around the room. He threw it to some of the other boys who passed it back to him. Mark was pleased to see that Charlie was not very happy seeing his football being passed around the room. The ball was just leaving Mark's hands in a passing move to Leroy when Mr Parkins came in.

"What are you doing, Mark? You know you're supposed to find something quiet to do during a wet playtime. Whose ball is it?" he asked as he put his hand out to take it from Mark.

Charlie put his hand up. "Well, Charlie, you're new here so you didn't know that footballs should be kept in a box in the cloakrooms. As for you, Mark, you have a lunchtime detention on Monday."

When Charlie came back into the classroom after putting his football away, Mark glared at him. He whispered, "I'll get you for that." Charlie gave him a 'you're an idiot' look and got on with his work.

Mark is really against Charlie now. Is it fair? What do you think he means when he says "I'll get you for that"?

On Saturday mornings the boys usually met at the park for a kickabout. Tom, Leroy and the others were, as usual, being organised by Mark. Then Charlie arrived.

"Hi, Charlie. Do you want to join us?" asked Tom.

"He's not playing in our game!" shouted Mark.

"Why not?" asked Leroy.

"Because it's my football and I say who plays," announced Mark.

"That's not fair!" said Charlie. He was getting really fed up with Mark. He felt he was making an effort to mix with the boys in his new class. He didn't understand what Mark's problem was.

"What are you going to do about it?" shouted Mark. He dropped his football and stood in front of Charlie in a threatening way. There would be no teacher to interfere now!

"We can play with my football," retorted Charlie. But when he said that Mark lunged forward, knocked Charlie to the ground, then grabbed his football and kicked it away.

"That's what I think about your crummy little football," said Mark, glaring down at Charlie. The other boys stood around them, not knowing what to do.

Charlie got up and started to run after his ball. "Come on, get him!" shouted Mark. He started to run after Charlie – he wanted to beat him up. The other boys followed and when Charlie picked up his ball he saw a pack of wild boys chasing after him and so he ran away as fast as he could.

The chase was on, but Charlie was a natural athlete and was beginning to get away. Mark urged the others to run faster. They chased him past the swings and through the main gates of the park. Charlie got to the main road and stopped. The shopping centre was opposite and he knew if could get across the road he could lose the pack behind him. There were cars parked along either side of the road. He crept out from between two parked cars, looked both ways but the road was busy with shoppers. He heard Mark shouting behind him so he looked again, there was a slight gap in the traffic and he dashed across. It was close – one car honked at him, but he was across. He stood on the other side and looked at the others as they arrived at the road.

Mark stood there staring at Charlie. He really wanted to beat him up, to show him who was boss. Charlie stood there staring back, and then he smiled, waved and trotted off into the maze of shops.

"Come on, Mark," said Tom. "Leave him. Let's get back to our game."

But Mark had only one thing on his mind – to get Charlie. He started to cross the road. He looked one way, then the other, saw a gap in the traffic and began to run across the road. At the same time, a parked car pulled out and started to accelerate away.

The driver had been waiting to get out. There was a lot of traffic and he was getting impatient. He had seen a boy run across the road, nearly getting run over, and he thought how stupid some children were. He kept looking behind and when he finally saw a gap in the traffic he quickly put his foot on the accelerator and moved forward. Suddenly another boy was right in front of him. He slammed on the brakes but he was too late. There was a sickening thud and the boy flew on to the bonnet and crashed into the windscreen before sliding back down to the road. The driver quickly got out, afraid of what he was going to see.

Other cars had stopped and adults were rushing over to see what had happened. Tom and Leroy ran into the road to find Mark lying on his side in a pool of blood. When Charlie heard the screech of brakes he seemed to know what had happened and ran back and now he too stood helplessly staring at Mark. Someone must have telephoned for an ambulance because they all heard it approaching.

When the ambulance had left and the boys had given statements to the police they stood at the entrance to the park. Charlie turned to the others. "I'm really sorry. I don't know why he kept chasing me." He began to cry – the shock of seeing the accident was getting to him.

"It wasn't your fault," said Tom. "Mark is just like that."

"Do you think he's dead?" asked Leroy.

Mark was lucky. He had concussion and a nasty blow to the head. He also had a badly broken leg and three broken ribs, but at least he was alive. It would be a long time before he played football again.

Discussion:

1. How did Mark's own jealousy get him into danger?
2. Could the other boys have done more to stop Mark?
3. Crossing busy roads can be dangerous. How can you get across safely?
4. Think of ways of helping Charlie and Mark to be friends.

6
It Won't Hurt you

THEME: the dangers of taking Ecstasy

He was lying on the bathroom floor in a pool of his own sick. His eyes were closed and his body was twitching out of control.

What could have made this boy be unconscious? If you found somebody in this situation, what should you do?

Here is the whole story.

Rachel, Julie and Yasmin were standing at the corner, arguing about how to spend the next few hours. "Come on," urged Rachel, "let's go into town."

"But what are we going to do?" asked Julie.

"I think we should go to Harveys. It'll be a laugh," suggested Yasmin.

"They're all older kids. They won't like us being there," said Rachel.

"I keep telling you, it'll be all right," urged Yasmin. "You know Claire, Mark's older sister?" The others nodded. "I saw her this morning and she said we could come along."

"But what do they do at the back of Harveys?" asked Rachel.

Harveys was a derelict store that had a canopy at the back where lorries parked for deliveries. The local kids liked to hang out there because it was sheltered from the rain and was not overlooked from the street or other buildings.

Before Yasmin could answer, two older girls sauntered along. One was Claire. "Are you coming with us?" she asked the three friends. "It'll be wicked. Gary's bringing his CD player so we can have a bit of a disco."

"Yeh, we'll come," said Yasmin.

Rachel stood back as the others started off down the road. "I don't want to," she protested. She had heard that things went on there. At least, that's what her mother had said one day when she told Rachel never to go to such places.

Yasmin turned around and walked up to Rachel. "Look, we're all friends, we do things together. Nothing's going to happen to you. It'll only be for an hour. Come on!"

Rachel looked at all the others staring at her, waiting for her to make her mind up. She shrugged her shoulders and followed Yasmin.

How does Rachel feel at this moment? What is peer group pressure?

The five girls wandered out of the estate into an industrial area where there were a number of derelict buildings. As they approached Harveys they could hear music playing loudly. They rounded the corner at the back of Harveys and saw several teenagers sitting around, listening to the music and watching a couple of boys break-dancing. The three younger friends felt a sense of excitement. They had all heard about Harveys, and now they were going to be there themselves. Though they felt nervous they also felt comforted that Claire was with them to make sure no harm would come to them. Rachel couldn't help thinking about what her mum would say if she were to find out.

"Why d'yuh bring 'em?" asked a girl they recognised from their estate as Louise. She was known to be tough and fearless and when she approached them they all shrank back.

"They're all right. You won't say noth'n, will yuh?" said Claire, turning to the girls. They noticed she now talked in the same slangy way.

"Well, keep 'em away from me, snotty little toe-rags."

Claire and her friend joined the other teenagers while the three younger girls sat in a corner away from the others and watched. The girls were a bit disappointed, there was nothing going on here that they didn't see at the rec. A group of teenagers getting together, listening to music, sometimes dancing, talking, shouting, one couple snogging. Then Louise started circulating around the group, selling something. She had a small bag and it looked as though she was selling little white pills. She was collecting pound coins and notes from the others, depending on how many tablets they bought. Not all the teenagers bought a tablet – they noticed Claire and her friend didn't.

"What do you think she's selling?" asked Rachel.

"I bet they're Ecstasy tablets," said Yasmin.

"Aren't they bad for you?" questioned Julie.

"I don't know," said Yasmin. "My dad says they make you ill. But if they make you ill why do they take them? Look out, she's coming over here!"

Louise wandered over to the three girls. "Wanna try some? It won't hurt you."

"We haven't got any money," said Julie.

"Look, I'll tell yuh what I'll do," she leaned forward, nearly whispering. "You can 'av one for free, just to see if you like it. If you do you know where to come back for more. But don't let the others know – I'll 'av a riot on me 'ands if they knew I was givin' the stuff away free."

She held out the bag for the girls to take a tablet. Yasmin and Julie reached in but Rachel stood firm and said no.

"Go on, put it in yer mouth," urged Louise to Yasmin and Julie. Julie slowly put it in but just as Yasmin was about to, Louise was called by one of her friends. She left them to go and sell tablets to the others.

Julie had swallowed hers but Yasmin stopped and put the tablet into her pocket. Soon the mood began to change around the group. Those who didn't take a tablet started to wander away, while the others began to dance about in slow, rhythmic ways. Their speech became slurred as if they were drunk and some sat down, rocking to and fro. A couple began to drink quite heavily as if they had a great thirst and started to demand more.

Claire walked over to the girls and said, "I think we'd better go." The girls didn't argue but as they got up Julie suddenly staggered and was violently sick, splattering the other girls' shoes.

"Oh, for God's sake!" shouted Claire's friend, trying to jump back but too late. She stomped off, Claire following behind her.

Rachel and Yasmin stood either side of Julie and took one arm each, helping her to walk forward. Julie was lucky, she had brought up most of the tablet and what little was left in her system only made her feel very dizzy and thirsty. It seemed a long walk back to the estate. Julie began to cry and said she didn't want her parents to know. When they got to her front door she was feeling a bit better, at least well enough to get in the house, tell her mum she was feeling tired and go to her room for a lie down. She hadn't thought about what she was going to say to her mum when she discovered Julie's clothes covered in sick.

Once Julie was inside, Yasmin turned to Rachel. "Look, I can't take this into my house," she said, holding the tablet. "My dad's a policeman. He'd do his nut if he caught me with this!"

"You should have thought of that back there," argued Rachel.

"Will you take it, please?"

"No way! I could get into trouble as well, you know!"

"Look, all you have to do is take it to your bathroom and flush it down the loo. Please, Rachel, you're my best friend – please do this for me!"

Rachel reluctantly took the tablet and quickly put it into her pocket. The girls walked to the end of the street without talking and when they parted Yasmin again said thanks.

When Rachel got home she was determined to go straight to the downstairs bathroom and flush the tablet away.

"Oh, there you are, Rachel," said her mum, who was obviously in a hurry. "Mavis has gone home ill, so they want me down at the shop and I can't find my keys anywhere. Can I have yours?"

Rachel put her hand into her pocket and brought out her keys. They were attached to a small furry teddy bear keyring. Neither of them noticed a white tablet fall out of her pocket on to the floor.

Her mother rushed out of the door, telling her to give her little brother, Thomas, his tea. Rachel quickly went into the bathroom to flush the tablet away. But when she felt in her pocket she couldn't find it. She frantically searched all her pockets, but it was nowhere to be found. She couldn't believe it!

While she was in the bathroom her brother came into the lounge. He had been in his room, playing with his cars. He had only just turned four and he had a lot of new toys to play with. But he was bored now and he wanted to see what Rachel was doing. As he crossed the hall his eye was caught by a small white thing on the floor. He bent down to pick it up, examined it and, deciding it was a sweet, popped it into his mouth.

At that moment Rachel came out of the bathroom. She didn't look at Thomas but began searching the floor. Thomas wandered over to the toilet – he was feeling a bit funny and he thought he needed to go to the loo.

Rachel searched the floor – she was sure the tablet must have fallen out of her pocket when she gave her mother the keys. Perhaps it had rolled into a corner. She felt around the edge of the carpet. After a few minutes she heard a retching sound in the bathroom and she raced to the door, shouting, "Thomas?"

Thomas was lying on the bathroom floor in a pool of his own sick. His eyes were closed and his body was twitching out of control. Having seen the effect the Ecstasy tablet had on Julie, Rachel knew exactly what had happened. She raced over to him, his body was hot to the touch. She froze, not knowing what to do. Then suddenly she ran to the telephone and dialled 999. "Help! I need an ambulance!" she shouted to the operator. "My brother has taken a tablet and he's been sick and he's burning up!"

The operator got her to calm down, then asked her address and told her that an ambulance would be along in a few minutes. She told Rachel to turn Thomas on his side and make sure he wasn't choking on his own vomit.

Rachel ran back to the bathroom. Thomas was still twitching but his breathing made a rasping sound. She turned him on to his side, looked into his mouth but it was clear. His breathing became easier and Rachel began to sob, almost shouting at Thomas to get better.

The ambulance was only a few minutes, though it seemed like hours to Rachel. When she heard the ambulance she realised the front door was locked and ran to open it. The paramedics came rushing in and followed Rachel to the bathroom. They put an oxygen mask over Thomas's face to help him breathe and then carried him out to the waiting ambulance.

"What do you think he has eaten?" one of them asked.

Rachel began to cry again. "Come on, we haven't got much time. I need to know so the doctors will know how to treat him!" So Rachel told him about the Ecstasy tablet.

A neighbour had raced over when she saw the ambulance and Rachel went back to her house, where the neighbour telephoned her mother at the shop. Rachel had some explaining to do when she saw her mother later that evening.

Thomas was lucky – he was in hospital for three days but soon he made a full recovery. If Rachel hadn't called 999 right away he would not have survived. Of course, if Rachel and her friends hadn't done a number of things none of this would have happened.

Discussion:

1. What could Rachel have done to avoid Thomas's accident? What will her parents think about what happened?
2. What should happen now about the tablets being taken at the back of Harveys?
3. What kinds of drugs are harmful and what kinds are helpful to us? What about the long-term effects of taking drugs?
4. How can we keep drugs away from young children?

(Discuss the fact that young children can be violently affected by a drug because they have such a small body mass compared to an adult.)

7
Will You Be My Friend?

THEME: the risks of the internet chat room

"*My car is just over there. I could take you home to meet her. You could have tea together and then I could drive you back.*"

"*Oh, I don't know,*" *she said, trying to move away from him. But his hand tightened on her shoulder. She began to feel uncomfortable being near this man. She took another step back from him but he shifted his hand to her arm, gripping her tightly.*

"*Come on, don't be like that. Charlotte really wants to meet you.*"

How do you think this girl has got herself into this situation? Do you think Charlotte really exists?

Here is the whole story.

"Are you going on the net tonight?" asked Yasmin. She was walking home from school with her friends Julie and Rachel.

"Mum's going round to my nan's tonight and she said I had to go with her," replied Rachel.

"That's a shame you have to go, too," said Yasmin. "We could have had a good chat on the net."

"Nan's not very well so Mum said I should help cheer her up."

"What about you, Julie?" asked Yasmin.

"It depends if my brother is using the computer. Mum said he has priority because he has exams soon."

The girls reached the corner, where they went off in different directions, each to their own home. They waved goodbye to each other, Yasmin calling that she would be on-line at seven o'clock.

That evening Yasmin logged on and she was soon in contact with the usual group of girls, except Rachel and Julie. Yasmin slowly typed in answers to questions from the others and asked some herself. Then a new name came on-line – her name was Charlotte. Charlotte was new to the area and wanted to make friends. She seemed friendly enough and asked if anyone would like to meet her in town on Saturday, but nobody said they would.

Why were Yasmin and the others sensible not to agree to meet Charlotte?

While Yasmin was on-line, Rachel was racing to get back home. The visit to her nan didn't go too well as her nan had been ill and very quickly got tired. Rachel hoped her dad wasn't on the computer because she wanted to get on to the chat room. She was new to all this and found it fascinating that she could talk to a range of other people through the computer. Even though she had just spent the whole day with her friends at school she still wanted to chat to them.

Her heart sank when she got home and found her dad using the computer. "How long will you be?" she asked.

"I've just got this letter to finish, probably twenty minutes," he replied. "I'll give you a shout when I've done."

It was nearly nine o'clock before Rachel managed to get on to the computer and she was disappointed when she couldn't contact any of her friends. She was just about to log off when a new girl made contact – her name was Charlotte.

Charlotte: Hello, Rachel. My name is Charlotte. Will you stay on for a while and speak to me?

Rachel: Hello, Charlotte. Yes, I'll speak to you.

Charlotte: Oh good, I'm new to this. How old are you and where do you live?

Rachel: I've just turned eleven and I live in Newton city. What about you?

Charlotte: Wow! You won't believe this, but I'm eleven this weekend and I've just moved to Newton. I don't know anybody here. Will you be my friend?

Rachel: Yes, I'll be your friend. What school will you be going to?

Charlotte: I don't know yet. Maybe we can meet and you can tell me about your school. You sound really nice.

Rachel: Yes, we could meet. I'll bring my friends as well. You could join us for a burger in town.

Charlotte: I'm a bit shy with strangers. Could we meet on our own for the first time? I could meet your friends another time. I like the idea of a burger. As it's my birthday, I could treat you.

Rachel: That's really nice of you. I'll have to ask my parents first.

Charlotte: Tell them you're meeting your friends. You know what parents can be like!

Rachel: OK. Mum usually lets me go into town on my own.

Charlotte: That's great! I'm so excited. I'm so glad I've made contact with a new friend. What do you look like? How will I recognise you?

Rachel: I've got blond hair and blue eyes. I'll be wearing jeans and a bright red jacket. What do you look like? Should we meet outside McDonald's?

Charlotte: I'm quite short with long dark hair. I'll be wearing a blue jacket. I don't know where it is. I know where the car park is. What about at the entrance to that? At nine-thirty?

Rachel: That's not far from McDonald's. I'll meet you there at nine-thirty.
Charlotte: OK. That sounds great. I'm really going to have a nice birthday. Bye.

The next day Rachel was just about to leave to catch the nine o'clock bus.

"Where are you going?" asked her dad, who was on the computer again checking his e-mails.

"I'm going into town to meet Julie and Yasmin," lied Rachel.

"Don't forget to be back by lunchtime. We have to go to see Gran again," said Dad, without taking his eyes from the screen.

Rachel ran to catch the bus. She wasn't sure if she was doing the right thing. She was allowed to go into town on her own but only if she was meeting Yasmin and Julie. Charlotte had suggested lying to her parents – she wasn't sure why. But Charlotte did sound nice and if she wasn't there Julie decided she would come straight home.

She got off at the stop just a few metres from the car park. She was feeling rather nervous now and was beginning to have doubts about whether she should be there. She looked around but there was no short long-haired girl in a blue coat. She was almost relieved – after all, what if she didn't like Charlotte?

"Hello. You must be Rachel," said a voice behind her. She turned round to face a tall man wearing black jeans and a blue jacket. "I'm Charlotte's dad. She's not well but she asked me to meet you."

When Paul, Rachel's dad, finished checking his e-mails he thought he would look at something else on the net. He saw that Rachel had been on the chat room the evening before. He didn't like to pry into his daughter's chats but curiosity got the better of him and he logged in under her name. Her password was easy to guess – it was the name of her teddy bear, Jasper. Then he was able to see the conversation Rachel had had with Charlotte.

Rachel said nothing. This wasn't what she was expecting. All she could say was, "Is she all right?"

"Oh yes. It's only a cold but her mum thought it best that she doesn't come out. She would really like to meet you."

"I would like to meet her," said Rachel.

The man put his hand on Rachel's shoulder. "My car is just over there, I could take you home to meet her. You could have tea together and then I could drive you back."

"Oh, I don't know," she said, trying to move away from him. But his hand tightened on her shoulder. She began to feel uncomfortable being near this man. She took another step back from him but he shifted his hand to her arm, gripping her tightly.

"Come on, don't be like that. Charlotte really wants to meet you."

"Let me go!" shouted Rachel.

Paul couldn't believe what he was reading. Was he being a neurotic father? Or was Rachel doing something dangerous?

"Bev!" he called to his wife. "Quickly! Come and have a look at this."

Bev heard the urgency in his voice and came in right away. She read the words he was pointing at on the screen. "Oh, Paul, what's she doing?"

Paul looked at his watch "It's ten past nine. If we hurry we could get to the car park by nine thirty."

They both ran out of the house and jumped into the car. "Here," Paul said as he passed his mobile to Bev, "telephone 999 and ask for the police. We might get stuck in traffic, but they should get there quickly."

The man gripped Rachel's arm even tighter. Then he put his other arm around her face to stifle her screams. A passer-by stopped to look, but the man said, "My daughter. She always gets like this when she doesn't get her own way."

"I should give her a good smack," said the passer-by and walked on.

Rachel was having trouble breathing, the man was really hurting her. She was being dragged towards a van, where another man had leapt out to open the back door. She felt her body lifted up and she kicked her feet wildly.

Just at that moment there was the piercing sound of sirens and the screeching of a car sliding to a halt. Rachel was flung to the ground as the man tried to jump into his van. All Rachel could see was a flurry of feet and she felt a huge sense of relief when she recognised the uniforms of several policemen as they wrestled the men out of the van.

"Rachel!" called a familiar voice. She jumped to her feet and ran into the out-stretched arms of her mum and dad.

Discussion:

1. Who was Charlotte?
2. What were the danger signals that Rachel missed when she was talking to Charlotte?
3. Why did Charlotte tell Rachel not to say anything to her parents?
4. What was the correct thing Rachel should have done?
5. What kind of information should you not give over the net?

8
The Fire

CONSEQUENCES

THEME: fire hazards in the home

The heat was overpowering as the flames leapt at him. He couldn't breathe – the thick acrid smoke choked him. He tried to run out of the room but he tripped over a chair and banged his head on the dining table. He collapsed to the floor, almost unconscious and barely able to breathe in the oxygen he needed.

How do you think this fire in the house could have started? What will happen if the fire engine is late in arriving?

Here is the whole story.

Leroy was a boy in a hurry. He was supposed to meet his friends in town by ten o'clock and he was going to miss the bus.

"Don't forget your jacket. It's going to rain today," his mother shouted as he ran out of the door. He raced around the corner just in time as the bus pulled up. He hopped on, paid his fare and then flopped down on the first available seat.

Leroy was meeting Tom and Mark at the opening of the new sports shop. They were advertising the Manchester United away strips for half price and the boys thought it would look cool if they all had one for the five-aside competition at the sports centre that evening. They were in the same team as Gary and David, who already had the strips, so if the other three got the same strip then they wouldn't have to wear those silly bib-like tops the organisers make you wear.

The bus stopped just outside the precinct and when Leroy jumped off the bus he felt the first drops of rain fall on his head. He smiled to himself – his mother was always right about the weather. He put on his anorak and ran the full length of the precinct to where the new sports shop was.

"What kept you?" demanded Tom impatiently as Leroy came running up to them, puffing hard.

"Sorry," said Leroy. "Mum and Dad are going out tonight and she wanted to show Errol and I what we could cook for dinner."

"Is your brother bringing you to the football tonight?" asked Mark.

"If his car passes its MoT – otherwise we'll have to bus it."

"Can he give us a lift? Tom and I can come round to your place," suggested Mark.

"OK, I'll give you a call if he's got the car back."

Just as they finalised the arrangements for the evening the shopkeeper unlocked the doors of the sports shop and several boys raced in to find their favourite teams' football strips. The three friends gave whoops of delight as they found the away strip for Manchester United, but then moaned in disappointment when they realised all the shirts were in extra large size.

"Look at this!" exclaimed Tom, the first to put a shirt on. The arms were far too long and his hands had disappeared completely. He frantically looked for a smaller size but there weren't any.

"No wonder they're half price!" said Mark, who also had disappearing hands. Then he and Tom laughed hysterically as Leroy tried his shirt on. Leroy was shorter than the other two so the shirt looked even bigger on him. In fact, it looked so big that if he'd been a girl it could have been a dress!

But this did not deter the boys – they would roll up the sleeves and tuck the shirts into their shorts. They were used to having clothes too big for them, as their mothers always said "they would grow into them". Tom and Mark decided to wear theirs, while Leroy put his into a bag. He wasn't so sure about the wisdom of buying something so much the wrong size.

After a drink at the cafe the boys parted company and said they would meet later at Leroy's house as long as his brother's car was back.

Errol was sitting with his feet up watching television when Leroy came in. "Did your car pass its MoT?" he asked his brother.

"It sure did," Errol replied. "I can drop you off at the sports centre if you want."

"Can Tom and Mark come too?"

"Yeah, should be able to fit them in," said Errol.

"Thanks, that's brill!" said Leroy. He phoned the others to say that the lift was on. And he invited them to tea – it was pizzas and his mum had left enough to feed an army. Then he sat down with his brother to watch TV. It seemed that the weather was getting worse – he could hear rain pounding on the roof.

At about five o'clock the doorbell rang and when Leroy opened it he saw two very wet, bedraggled boys. They came into the house and shook themselves like dogs to get the water off their heads. Neither of them had a jacket on, they were too proud to cover up their new football tops.

"You're soaked through," said Leroy. Tom and Mark just grinned. "Do you want to take them off? I'll put them in the airing cupboard to dry."

The boys took off their wet tops and Leroy handed them a couple of sweatshirts belonging to Errol. As they put them on he opened the airing cupboard door. "They won't dry in time if you put them in there," said Errol. "Here, give them to me, I'll put them by the fire in the lounge. You go and get the pizzas out of the oven."

Errol took the two wet tops into the lounge. He put the electric fire on and while the bars turned red hot he dragged a couple of chairs over to the fire. He draped the football tops over the chairs so that they faced the fire and got the full blast of the heat. "That'll get them dried quickly," he muttered to himself. Then he went into the kitchen, where Leroy was serving out the pizzas.

They were enjoying the pizzas and talking about the five-aside competition that evening. The local church organised it every month and the boys had won the competition at least twice in the last year. They thought they would look really wicked in their new tops.

Meanwhile, in the lounge the fire was certainly drying the tops quickly. One of the shirts began to slip off the chair. Soon it had fallen down clear of the chair towards the electric fire. The body of the shirt dropped in front of the fire but one sleeve fell across the red-hot bars. Within seconds flames sprang into life and began to devour the shirt. Quickly the flames spread, looking for other things to feed on as they leapt about the room.

"Do you think they're dry yet?" asked Tom.

"Might be. Go and have a look," suggested Errol.

Tom got up and went out of the kitchen and down the hall to the lounge. The lounge door was closed and as he was just about to open it he thought he could smell smoke. Oh no! He panicked, thinking his shirt was about to go up in flames. He opened the door and rushed in but he couldn't see his shirt because the whole room was an inferno. The heat was overpowering as the flames leapt at him. He couldn't breathe – the thick acrid smoke choked him. He tried to run out of the room but he tripped over a chair and banged his head on the dining table. He collapsed to the floor, almost unconscious and barely able to breathe in the oxygen he needed.

The flames sucked in the air from the open door with a loud whoosh. And it was that sudden roar that brought the other boys running to the lounge door. Errol shielded his face and looked into the room. He could see Tom lying on the floor, not far from the door. "Stay there!" he shouted at the others. He took a deep breath of fresh air then ran into the room, grabbed Tom and dragged his unconscious body out. He fell in a heap on the hall floor, shouting at Leroy to close the lounge door.

Errol realised they must phone the fire service – but the phone was in the lounge. His mobile! Where was it? Not in the lounge as well? No, it was in his coat pocket, hanging over a chair in the kitchen. "Come on!" he shouted at the others as he staggered to the kitchen. Leroy and Mark dragged Tom and by the time they got him into the kitchen and through the side door into the drive, Errol had finished his call and the firemen were racing for their machine.

It took only a few minutes for the fire engine to reach the house. Luckily, as the boys had kept the lounge door closed the damage to the house was confined to that room. The whole house got very smoky, though, and eventually needed cleaning and decorating.

As for Tom, he was lucky. He regained consciousness as soon as the others dragged him outside. But he still went to hospital for a check-up. He had a headache from bumping his head on the dining table and sore lungs from inhaling smoke. He was allowed home the next day after having a comfortable night. He was lucky that Errol acted so quickly, but of course if Errol hadn't been so stupid in the first place Tom would have been playing football in his new shirt instead of lying in hospital.

Discussion:

1. What was the stupid thing Errol did that was so dangerous?
2. When Tom got to the lounge door why was he wrong to open it?
3. How would the story be different if there had been smoke alarms in the lounge?
4. What other fire dangers must we watch out for around the house?

CONSEQUENCES

9
Let's Go for a Ride

THEME: the dangers of cycling without a helmet

He raced around the corner, desperate to be first. He looked behind him and laughed because he was way ahead. When he turned his head to look at the road in front he suddenly saw a large white van in the middle of the road. He tried to squeeze the brakes on and though his tyres locked he was going too fast – he just kept going.

Why do you think he was going fast? What is going to happen?

Here is the whole story.

"I'm bored," said Leroy for the third time in the last half-hour.

"We wouldn't be bored if you hadn't kicked the ball into old Grumpy's garden," Tom told him.

They didn't know the man's real name, but they called him Grumpy because he was always complaining whenever the football hit his fence. This time Leroy had kicked the ball over the fence and Grumpy quickly came outside to get it and told them they wouldn't get it back. Ashley was furious because it was his ball and he had only got it last week. Ashley had shouted at Grumpy that he would get his dad over to get the ball back. Grumpy just made a rude sign at them and went indoors with the ball.

So the boys were now sitting under the big tree in the park, wondering what to do. They were throwing pebbles and bits of stick into Tom's upturned cycle helmet. He was the only one who wore a helmet. Leroy lost his and didn't have the nerve to tell his parents. Mark and Ashley never wore a helmet. When Tom first turned up at the park with one they teased him but Tom just ignored them and they soon didn't bother to say anything. Tom's helmet was now a part of his gear, and, it made a good target for throwing pebbles into.

What is the purpose of wearing a cycle helmet?

"Let's go for a ride," suggested Mark.

"It's too hot," said Tom.

"I know," suggested Leroy, "we could have a race around the field." Leroy was always competitive; he had to turn everything they did into a competition. It was his idea to throw things into Tom's helmet and he kept a score as to who succeeded in throwing the most pebbles into the helmet. He got bored once he knew he wasn't winning. The other boys didn't like the idea of racing.

"Let's go down to Old Mill stream," proposed Mark. "We could build a dam." He also liked the idea of paddling in the cold water to cool himself down. All the boys perked up at that idea. They hadn't been down there for some time, especially since the heavy rains had made the stream overflow. But the weather had been very dry over the last few weeks and the stream was probably just right for messing about in.

The boys picked up their bicycles and began to cycle towards the exit of the park. "Wait for me!" shouted Tom, who was trying to get all the pebbles and bits of stick out of his helmet before putting it on. With his helmet secured on his head, he furiously peddled to catch up with the others.

Old Mill stream was situated in a valley covered by woods. The valley was surrounded by housing estates and was a popular place for the locals to walk. Because the valley was steep the road took a winding route down and in places was only wide enough for one car.

On leaving the park the boys rode along a busy main road then after about half a mile turned into the estate. They were going past the road where Ashley lived. "Hang on, I want to go home and get some sweets," he shouted. The other boys followed him to his house and waited outside while he went in. He went to the sweet jar and put a handful of brightly wrapped sweets into his pocket. After a quick drink of water he rejoined his friends.

The boys carried on through the estate towards the top of the valley through which the Old Mill stream flowed. It was called that because at the head of the valley there used to be a flour mill; now there was just an old ruin. As they cycled along they chatted to each other.

"Are you going to watch Match of the Day tonight?" asked Mark to nobody in particular.

"Are you allowed to stay up late?" asked Tom.

"When my mum and dad are out the sitter usually lets me," said Mark.

"My mum says I don't need a sitter now," said Ashley.

"You're lucky," said Leroy. "My parents will leave me for an hour but if they're going out for a long time I have to stay with my gran – it's so boring." Leroy was going through a stage when he found most things boring!

The boys reached the top of the valley. Here, the road narrowed slightly as it wound its way down to the stream. Leroy suddenly shouted, "I'll race you to the bottom!" and he set off quickly down the lane.

Tom and Mark stayed behind – they didn't like the fast speed down this steep road. But Ashley rose to the challenge and raced after Leroy. Soon they were both side by side, shooting down the road.

"Come on, slow coach!" shouted Leroy as he went ahead.

That made Ashley angry. Leroy was a good friend but his competitiveness irritated his friends. When he was winning he gloated and when he was losing he pretended to be bored as if he didn't care. Ashley put on a spurt and caught him up – he was determined to beat Leroy, especially as it was Leroy who'd lost his football.

Down in the valley Mike put his van into a lower gear as he began to climb up the lane. He had just finished a hard day's work at the old mill. The mill now had new owners who were restoring it with the intention of turning it back into a working mill. Mike was a carpenter and he was putting in the new windows. He leaned forward to turn his radio on, momentarily taking his eye off the road. He found Radio 1 and then concentrated on the task of driving around the bends that would lead him out of the valley.

Ashley and Leroy were now building up quite a speed. Leroy was beginning to panic as he nearly came off at a bend. He slowed down as he came into another bend and, much to his annoyance, he saw Ashley shoot on ahead of him. Ashley gave a whoop of joy as he leapt ahead of Leroy. He raced around the corner, desperate to be first. He looked behind him and laughed because he was way ahead. When he turned his head to look at the road in front he suddenly saw a large white van in the middle of the road. He tried to squeeze the brakes on and though his tyres locked he was going too fast – he just kept going.

Mike panicked when his mobile phone rang. He was so tired he had forgotten where he had put it. He looked down at the front passenger seat and found it under his coat. He put the telephone to his ear at the same time as his eyes returned to look at the road ahead. What he saw made him drop the telephone, grip the steering wheel and slam his breaks on as hard as he could. The road was too narrow for him to swerve to one side. Before he came to a halt there was a loud crash as the cyclist hurtled into the front of his van. He was aware of a body flying into his windscreen and then he couldn't see anything as the glass shattered into thousands of pieces. When the van stopped he instantly jumped out, dreading what he was going to see.

Leroy heard the screeching brakes and the impact before he rounded the corner. He was already applying his brakes to stop so when he came up to the van he was hardly moving. He stood there, one foot on the ground, both hands on the handle-bars, watching the driver get out of his van and run around to look at Ashley. The other two boys came round the corner and quickly stopped. All the boys dropped their bicycles and ran to the scene.

Ashley was very still and there was blood flowing from his head. Mike ran back to his van to find his mobile phone and call for an ambulance. Leroy couldn't look at Ashley's still body. All he could stare at were some brightly coloured sweets scattered across the road.

(Note from the author: This story is dedicated to a twelve-year-old boy I used to teach who died from a similar accident. He, too, was not wearing a helmet. It was the saddest funeral I had ever been to.)

Discussion:

1. How do you think Leroy was feeling at the end of the story?
2. Do you think Mike, the van driver, should be feeling guilty?
3. What can be learnt about road safety from this story?

(It is impossible to say whether Ashley would have survived if he had been wearing a helmet. He certainly would have had a better chance of survival. Talk about other activities, such as skateboarding, where protective clothing should be worn.)

10

CONSEQUENCES

He Told Me to Do It!

THEME: **being coerced into doing something wrong**

Suddenly the roof gave way and he fell through in a shower of broken plastic. He hit the concrete floor and immediately felt a searing pain in his ankle.

Why would someone be climbing on a plastic roof? What are the dangers of such an act?

Here is the whole story.

When Leroy got up that morning he thought it was the most exciting day of his life! At last he was going to be in the starting line-up for the school football team. Gary had been away all week with the flu, so Mr Parkins said Leroy could start the game instead of being a sub yet again. Leroy was ecstatic. He was determined to show Mr Parkins how well he could play and then maybe he would be a regular in the team.

He could barely eat his breakfast because of the excitement, especially when Errol, his elder brother, said he would come and watch. Leroy grabbed his rucksack, threw in his lunchbox and his new football boots and ran out of the door without even saying goodbye to his parents, who were sitting at the breakfast table wondering what the whirlwind was!

When Leroy got to school he met up with the other boys. They too couldn't talk about anything other than the football match after school. What made them even more excited was when Mr Parkins said the pitch was dry enough for them to go on at lunchtime and that they could practise taking free kicks and corners.

When lunchtime came the boys wolfed down their sandwiches and raced outside. They all went out without changing, except for Leroy. He was hopeless at taking deadball kicks unless he was wearing his football boots so he took off his trainers and put his boots on. There was one other thing he was hopeless at – that was tying his laces up so that they would stay tied. By the time he got outside the lace of his right boot was already becoming loose.

At first the boys were very sensible and were organised with their practising.

Then Mark and some of the others began to dribble and pass the ball between them and taunt the others to catch them and soon a rather disorganised game started. Leroy didn't know what side he was on but he just enjoyed chasing after whoever had the ball. He was chasing hard when the ball slid away from Tom and rolled towards Leroy. He lined the ball up and took a wild kick at it, but the ball bounced up from a lump in the grass and Leroy missed. By this time his bootlace had come completely undone and trailed behind him. He was unaware of this and when he missed the ball his football boot shot off his foot. At first he fell over laughing hysterically, then he shouted in dismay as he watched his boot fly on to the roof of the swimming pool changing rooms.

He got up and ran over to the low, flat-roofed building. The roof was covered in thin, corrugated plastic and the boys were always getting told off for kicking a ball up there.

"What did you do that for?" asked Tom.

"I didn't do it deliberately!" retorted Leroy. "Let's ask Mrs Baker if she can get it."

They ran over to the dinner lady and told her what had happened, but she was not very sympathetic. "We keep telling you to tie your laces up properly, Leroy, but you never listen."

"Please, Mrs Baker, I need my boot for the match tonight," pleaded Leroy.

"Even if I wanted to I couldn't go climbing ladders – that's not in my job description. You'll have to wait until the caretaker comes in after school." She walked away to deal with a younger child who had fallen over.

"What am I going to do?" cried Leroy. "Mr Parkins won't let me play if I don't have my boots!"

"Mr Eaton will get it down after school," said Mark.

"How do we know if he'll be here on time?" Leroy was now getting very upset. Then Tom had an idea, "Come on, follow me!" He led the boys to the back of the swimming pool. He waited until there were no dinner ladies watching and then dashed along the side of the pool that was against the school fence. There was just enough space for them to sneak along.

"We're not supposed to be here. It's against school rules," whispered Leroy.

"Look, do you want to get your boot or not?" Leroy didn't answer – Tom seemed to know what he was doing. They stopped at the other side of the changing room, hidden from view.

"All you've got to do is climb up there, get your boot and climb down again," explained Tom.

"No way!" exclaimed Leroy. "I'm not going up there. What about the dinner ladies?"

"They won't see you if you keep your head down," encouraged Mark. "You're smaller than us – we can lift you up."

"Come on, Leroy. Are you chicken?" taunted Tom.

Leroy was always struggling to be accepted by the others because he was smaller than them. And he was desperate to be in the match so he said, "All right, but don't drop me!"

Tom and Mark cupped their hands for Leroy to step on to and when he put his right foot down they hoisted him up. He scrambled on to the edge of the roof and rested to get his bearings. He could see his boot, right in the middle of the roof. The roof was clear corrugated plastic and he could see into the changing rooms below. The plastic was beginning to go yellow with age and there were cracks in it because it was going brittle. But Leroy didn't notice that – his eyes were focused on his boot as he eased himself further on to the roof.

He thought it would be quicker if he stood up and stepped across. Suddenly the roof gave way and he fell through in a shower of broken plastic. He hit the concrete floor and immediately felt a searing pain in his ankle.

Tom and Mark couldn't see what had happened but they heard the crash of broken plastic and Leroy's scream. They dashed out from the behind the changing rooms and ran to Mrs Baker. At first she couldn't understand what had happened but then she ran indoors to get Mr Parkins and also a key for the changing room door.

As the two adults opened the door they could hear Leroy whimpering inside. They found him lying on his side holding his ankle and crying that it hurt. He had blood on his face from a number of little cuts made by the shattered plastic.

"You'd better go and ring for an ambulance, Mrs Baker. I think he has a broken ankle," said Mr Parkins. "I think we'll just wait here for the ambulance. The paramedics can check you over to make sure you haven't broken anything else. What on earth do you think you were doing up there?"

"I wanted to get my football boot. I accidentally kicked it on to the roof," whimpered Leroy.

"But that was a very silly thing to do!"

"It was Tom's idea. He told me to do it."

Tom and Mark shrank back, hoping Mr Parkins wouldn't notice them, but they were out of luck because he did see them and said, "I'll see you two later!"

Leroy was lucky, all he broke was his ankle. It was in plaster for several weeks, which meant that his football season was over. Tom and Mark were also banned from football for the rest of the term.

Discussion:

1. Leroy knew that what he was doing was wrong, so why did he do it?
2. Is it an acceptable excuse to say that somebody told you to do something?
3. How should you respond if someone else suggests doing something you know is dangerous?
4. Was it right that Tom and Mark should have been punished? Why?/Why not?
5. When Leroy has the cast taken off his ankle what is the first thing he has to learn?

11
The Railway Line

THEME: the dangers of playing on a railway line

He was aware of the others frantically waving and shouting, but he was concentrating on timing his leap as the train got nearer. He felt a sense of exhilaration as the great thunderous monster bore down on him.

Why would this boy want to stand in front of a train like this? What is he trying to prove?

Here is the whole story.

Julie and her friends were lazing about in her back garden. Rachel and Yasmin were there and they had been practising shooting at a netball post, when Tom, Mark and David, Mark's cousin, arrived.

"Neat netball post," said Tom in admiration. "Can I take some shots?" He didn't wait for Julie to reply, but grabbed the ball and started to shoot at the ring at the top of the post. The netball post was in the middle of a patch of grass in a small rectangular garden. The garden backed on to the main railway line, though you couldn't see it because of the high wooden fence around the perimeter.

The space was only big enough for taking shots, but soon a game of sorts started to take place, with the boys versus the girls. After a few minutes there was a roar and rumble as an intercity train raced by. All the children, except David, ignored it. David ran over to the fence and tried to jump up to see over.

"Wow! I didn't know you had a railway line behind your house," he exclaimed, feeling frustrated because he couldn't see over the high fence.

"It's only a railway line," replied Julie. "Haven't you seen one before?"

"Of course I have," said David indignantly. "I've got one near where I live. It's our favourite place to hide out, me and my mates."

"You're not supposed to go on the tracks," said Rachel. This was the first time the others had met David and Rachel thought he was a bit of a big head.

"It's all right, there's plenty of places to hide. It's cool being so close to the trains!"

"You're a nutter," said Rachel. She couldn't be bothered speaking to him any more.

"Come on," urged David to Mark and Tom. "Let's go over. It'll be great!"

Mark was ready to climb the fence but Tom stood back. "No!" he said. "Mum would ground me if she found out."

"You're just a chicken!" mocked David.

"Look, are you boys playing or not?" asked Julie, sensing Tom and David were about to start a fight. "We're winning, you know."

Julie tried to pass the ball to Yasmin but Tom jumped up and intercepted it. He was quite glad to be playing netball again. He looked to pass the ball to Mark but Mark was being covered by Rachel so he threw it to David. It was a good throw but David took his eye off the ball and dropped it. The ball rolled to Rachel, who scooped it up, shot and scored. "Three nil!" shouted the girls with glee.

"Good one, David! Can't you even catch a ball?" scoffed Tom.

David didn't like being spoken to like that. He grabbed the ball from Rachel and threw it as hard as he could at Tom, so hard it was impossible for Tom to catch it. Tom tried to duck but the ball glanced off his head and sailed up into the air. All the children watched in dismay as it flew over the fence and down into the railway cutting.

"Good one, David!" shouted Julie. "I only got that ball last week!"

"He should have caught it!" shouted back David, pointing at Tom.

"Nobody could have caught that," protested Rachel.

David realised that they were all ganging up on him. Tom was a popular boy, especially with the girls. Even Mark was keeping quiet and not defending him. "I'll go and get your precious ball," he yelled. "Mark, give me a leg up." He stood by the back fence and Mark cupped his hands and hoisted David up and over the fence before any of the others could say anything.

Julie ran to the shed and got out garden chairs for the others to stand on. There were now five heads poking up over the fence, watching David scramble down the embankment. Julie kept looking behind her to make sure her mother didn't notice what was going on.

When David got to the bottom he looked around for the ball. He saw it in a ditch on the other side of the two sets of tracks. But before retrieving the ball he put his head down to the railway line. The children watched in fascination as he put his ear to the track. "What are you doing?" shouted Julie.

David stood up. "I'm listening for a train. You can hear them miles away. I think there's one coming." David stood in the middle of the track, looking down the line.

"He's an idiot," muttered Tom.

"Come on, David!" shouted Mark. "Get the ball!"

David stood there, waiting for the train to come round the bend. He was going to show them that he wasn't afraid. He'd jump out of the way when the train got close – he'd done it lots of times before. I bet that chicken Tom wouldn't do it, thought David.

They could all hear the train getting closer and within seconds they could see it. The driver must have seen David because he started to hoot his warning horn and apply the emergency brakes. David knew the train couldn't stop and poised himself ready to leap clear. He was aware of the others frantically waving and shouting, but he was concentrating on timing his leap as the train got nearer. He felt a sense of exhilaration as the great thunderous monster bore down on him. He timed it to perfection and leapt clear of the roaring engine.

But it was so loud, he didn't hear another train coming from the other direction. That was what the others were trying to warn him about!

(Note to the teacher: What happens next is up to you and how much impact you want the story to make. Here are two possible endings.)

(A)   David felt the shaking of the line before he heard the other train. He dived to the side, only just in time as the other train came roaring by with its whistle blaring. He lay in a patch of nettles, so shaken he didn't notice the stinging leaves. He had never been that close to death before and the experience made him shake suddenly and then be violently sick. He realised just how lucky he had been.

(B)   David swung round to face the oncoming train. He could see the driver frantically waving his arms. David could feel the force of the air in front of the train as he tried to dive clear. He nearly made it. His left leg was still over the line as the train roared past. At first he just felt a thump on his leg but when he raised himself up and looked down, he saw the lower part of his leg had been cleanly cut off. Then the pain hit him and he fainted.

Discussion:
1. Why was David trying to prove how brave he was?
2. What other dangers can there be on railway lines? (Mention objects thrown on to tracks.)
3. Why are trains more dangerous than other forms of transport, such as cars?

(Discuss the fact that they are on tracks so they can't swerve out of the way; they are very heavy so they take a long time to stop; they can go very fast, etc.)

12
The Building Site

*M*ike knocked the wooden support from the roof beams. It had done its job and was no longer needed. He was about to bang the nail out of the wood when the foreman shouted that his wife was on the telephone. She was expecting a baby any day now, so Mike dropped the piece of wood and ran across the site to the foreman's office and grabbed the phone. She had started to go into labour, she said, and wanted him home as soon as possible. Mike dashed to his car, while the foreman shouted out to him, wishing him good luck. When Mike had dropped the wooden support it had clattered down to the ground and there it rested, with the long sharp nail pointing up.

Why are pieces of wood with nails sticking out very dangerous? Why did Mike leave the nail in the wood?

Here is the whole story.

Tom was in trouble – he could tell by the look on his mum's face as she put the telephone down.

"That was Leroy's mother. Apparently it was your idea to go down to the building site at Morgan's Quay."

"No way! It was Mark who suggested going there."

"Well, whoever it was, she isn't pleased that Leroy has lost one of his trainers. Do you know anything about it?"

"We thought they were finished," Tom tried to explain, "but this man came running out, shouting we were trespassing. Leroy ran ahead and he stepped into this wet concrete and when he pulled his foot out his shoe was left behind."

"Leroy's mother wants to make sure you boys don't go to the building site again. They are dangerous places, so promise me you won't go there."

"All right, I promise," replied Tom – but, as it turned out, that promise was one he wasn't going to keep.

The next day was Saturday and the three boys met up at the park.

"My mum had to go down to the building site to get my trainer," said a sullen Leroy. He had obviously got into real trouble with his parents.

"Why did she have to phone my mum and why did you say it was my idea?" asked Tom.

"Sorry, I didn't think she'd phone you," said Leroy. Then he glared at Mark. "It was one of your stupid ideas."

"I wasn't the stupid one stepping into the wet concrete!" argued Mark. "I only wanted to get some wood for my model, you didn't have to come with me. And as I didn't get any I'm going back there now. Do you want to come?"

"No way!" declared both Leroy and Tom.

"Look, there's nobody there on a Saturday and you don't have to come in," responded Mark. "Are you scared that your mummies will find out?"

Tom and Leroy looked at each other – they hated being taunted by Mark. They agreed to go with him but only to wait outside the fence. It was a ten-minute cycle ride away and when they got to the area they first of all cycled right past to make sure that this time there were no workmen still there. When they were satisfied that there was nobody about they stopped by the fence. It wasn't a very secure fence and Mark easily climbed over. "Wait there. I know where there's some wood," he said.

Tom and Leroy kept looking around, hoping no one was about. They were alerted by Mark running up to the fence.

"You must come and see this. The concrete you stepped in has gone hard and you've left a massive footprint in it." And Mark ran off towards the half-finished houses.

Leroy couldn't resist having a look so he climbed the fence and ran after Mark. Tom didn't like being left alone so he also climbed over to join them. He ran up to where Leroy and Mark were pointing and laughing at the large footprint he'd left in the middle of the concrete path. They were wondering if it would stay there for ever when a shout boomed across the site: "Hey, what are you doing there?"

It was Mike. His rush from the site the day before had been a false alarm. He had returned to pick up some tools he had left behind in his hurry to get away. He began to walk quickly towards the boys, who started sprinting back to the fence. Tom didn't see the long piece of wood with the nail sticking out. As he put his foot down he could feel a sudden pain as the nail passed through the soft sole of his trainer and into his foot. He sat down, trying to hold his throbbing foot.

Leroy was behind him and saw what had happened. He grabbed the wood and pulled the nail from Tom's shoe. Then he helped Tom up and supported him as he hobbled towards the fence. Mike wasn't very fit for running and once he saw the boys leaving the site he stopped chasing them and went back to the office to collect his tools.

Mark and Leroy helped Tom over the fence, got on their bikes and cycled away, with Tom doing the best he could with only one good foot. When they were a few blocks away and it was obvious they were not being chased, they stopped and sat down by the side of the road.

"I still didn't get a piece of wood!" exclaimed Mark.

"How's your foot?" asked Leroy, seeing Tom hold his foot, trying to keep back the tears of pain.

"It hurts!" he shouted as he took off his shoe and sock to inspect the damage. He was surprised there wasn't much blood. He could see a small puncture hole where the nail had pierced his foot. Though it didn't look like much, it didn't half hurt!

"I did that once," said Mark. "It hurt for a while but it soon got better. My mum bathed it in hot water and put some antiseptic on it."

Tom thought that it might be a good idea if he did the same so he said goodbye to the other two and cycled home, pushing down on only one pedal. When he got home he limped into the house. His mum asked him what was wrong with his foot and he said he had twisted his ankle playing football. She said she should look at it but he said it would be OK and went upstairs. He went into the bathroom and after taking his shoe and sock off he ran warm water over his foot to clean it. When he'd dried it he put some antiseptic cream on it.

Over the next few days Tom kept cleaning the wound and putting antiseptic cream on it but it didn't seem to get better. In fact it was hurting even more and he noticed that his foot was swelling up. But still he didn't let his mother look at it. When she was around the house he tried to walk normally or stay sitting down. Luckily it was the school holidays so he spent a lot of time just sitting, watching TV.

After four days things turned dramatically worse. Not only was his foot hurting but the pain was slowly travelling up his leg. He was hot and didn't feel very hungry. His mum thought he was getting the flu. He became very shivery and then suddenly he fainted.

It was his dad who found him when he came home early from work. When he came into the lounge he saw Tom lying on the floor. He rushed over to him and could feel he was burning with a fever. He feared the worst – that Tom had meningitis, a disease that can be fatal. He picked up the telephone and dialled 999 for an ambulance and then he phoned his wife to ask her to come home right away.

When they got Tom to hospital the doctors also thought he might have meningitis. Then the nurse, who was changing Tom into a hospital gown, noticed his swollen foot and lower leg. She called the doctor over and he examined the foot and found the puncture hole made by the nail. Now he knew what the problem was.

"How did Tom hurt his foot?" asked the doctor.

"He said he sprained his ankle playing football," said Tom's mum.

"I can assure you that a sprained ankle wouldn't cause this infection. He has stepped on something. It looks as though it could be a nail or some other sharp object. Bacteria from this object has entered into his bloodstream and has poisoned his blood. We call it septicaemia."

"Can it be treated?" asked Tom's dad, looking very worried.

"Untreated, Tom would definitely die, but we have him here in time so with a course of strong antibiotics he should recover."

"Thank goodness for that," said both parents.

"I'm afraid that was the good news. The not-so-good news is that his foot is in a very bad way. It may have to be amputated, but we'll know better tomorrow. If we can start reducing the swelling then we might be lucky."

Tom was lucky. Because he was young and healthy his body responded very well to the antibiotics. Not only did his temperature start to come down the next day but his foot became less swollen over the next few days. He was in hospital for over a week but he made a full recovery. Once he was better his parents became very cross with him when he finally told them what had happened.

Discussion:

1. Why were Tom's parents very cross with him?
2. What other dangers are there on a building site?
3. How do builders make sure they are safe when they are working on a site?

(Discuss the issue about Tom not telling the truth about how he hurt his foot, how that delayed him getting the right treatment.)

13
The Yellow Dinghy

CONSEQUENCES

THEME: safety at the seaside

*S*he tried to paddle back towards the shore but her arms became heavy and she flopped with exhaustion. It was a losing battle as the wind, tide and current pushed her further out to sea. No one seemed to notice her feeble shouts.

What is happening here? How do you think this girl got herself into this situation? What could be the consequences if she is not rescued?

Here is the whole story.

"Do I have to go with you?" moaned Rachel as her parents loaded the car.

"Yes," replied her mother. "I'll have no more whingeing from you. I'll not have your moods ruin Thomas's birthday." This was said in such a way that Rachel knew there was to be no more complaining.

Thomas was going to be six and when his parents asked him what he would like to do for his birthday he said straight away that he would like to go to the beach. He asked if his best friend, Christopher, could go as well. Rachel asked if one of her friends could go too but her Dad said there wouldn't be room in the car. So not only was Rachel missing out on being with her friends on a sunny, warm Saturday afternoon, but she also had to sit in the back of the car with two horrible little boys.

Thomas sat in the middle of the back seat, with Chris and Rachel either side of him. Rachel didn't want to sit next to Chris – he always seemed to have a runny nose and today was no exception. The boys sat there excitedly, as Thomas opened his birthday present. It was a snorkel and mask – perfect for a trip to the seaside! Rachel lost interest within seconds and switched on her Walkman to listen to her latest CD.

The beach was beginning to get crowded when they arrived after an hour's journey. The boys were already in their swimming trunks so they kicked off their trainers and ran down to the water's edge to paddle. Mum and Dad emptied the car of all the usual beach equipment – windbreak, rugs, dinghy and coolbox containing birthday food. Rachel just stood there watching, wondering what she was going to do. Mum threw her a rug and she laid it out on the sand a few metres from the rest of the family. She didn't want to be seen sitting by a windbreak!

The boys came racing back. "Can we play with the dinghy?" asked Thomas.

"Wait until I blow it up," said Dad. It was only a small plastic dinghy, with just enough space for two small boys or one adult. He got out the foot pump and after a few minutes it was blown up. Thomas and Chris made a grab for it but Dad stopped them. "Wait a minute. Let's just see where you can play with it."

He walked down to the water's edge and the two boys followed him with the dinghy. There was an area marked off with ropes and buoys for swimming and large signs warning about the dangers of going beyond the ropes because of strong tides and currents. A lifeguard was telling off a group of older boys for swimming beyond the ropes.

"See those ropes?" said Dad. "You must stay within this area. I'll stay here and watch." The boys gave a whoop of delight and dashed into the water.

Rachel propped herself up on one elbow and watched the boys. It was getting very hot and the sea looked inviting. "Mum, did you pack my swimming suit?"

"Yes, I thought you might change your mind. Your suit and a towel are in that carrier bag."

Rachel reached for the bag and looked around for somewhere to change. "You'll have to change out here," said her mother, knowing what was going through Rachel's mind.

"I hate doing that," said Rachel, flouncing on to her rug again.

"Come on," coaxed her mum. "I'll hold the towel. You should have changed before coming out, like the boys."

"I didn't know I was going to go into the stupid water." Rachel stood up and while her mother held the towel she quickly changed.

"Go and have a good swim. The water might cool that temper of yours!"

Rachel wandered down to the water. There were lots of people there, swimming, playing on all types of inflatables, splashing each other and generally having a good time. Perhaps she was being a bit miserable – it wasn't fair on Thomas. She waded into the water and looked around for her brother.

She was about knee deep when her breath was taken away as cold water was splashed all over her – Thomas had found her! Thomas and Chris were sitting in the dinghy, leaning over to splash her and laughing hysterically.

"Stop it!" screamed Rachel. "I don't want to get my hair wet!" But that only made the boys splash more water at her. She had been grumpy towards them all day and this was their chance to get back at her. They really enjoyed seeing her get angry.

Rachel was in a fury now. The boys tried to paddle away but she was too quick. She grabbed the dingy with both hands and with a mighty pull turned it over so that both boys fell into the water. They came spluttering to the surface and Thomas shouted, "I'm telling Dad on you!"

But Dad just laughed and, seeing that Rachel was in the water with the boys, he strolled back to the windbreak to see if the picnic was ready – he was getting hungry.

Meanwhile, the boys tried to grab at the dinghy but Rachel pulled it away. She turned it over, jumped in and paddled away from the boys. "You can have the dinghy! I'm going to play with my snorkel!" Thomas shouted after her. Rachel floated to the edge of the swimming area. She noticed that some boys were playing on the other side of the ropes so she pushed the rope under the dinghy and drifted away from the swimming area.

Sam was really fed up. He had been on duty all morning without a break. There should have been three lifeguards working on the beach, but Lisa phoned in to say she was ill so that only left him and Jethro. As two had to be on duty at any one time that meant they couldn't have any breaks, so food and refreshments would have to be taken on duty. He was also having trouble with a group of boys who kept going out beyond the ropes. He noticed that they had gone beyond the marked-off area again and he would have to speak to them once more but that meant leaving his station. He couldn't do anything until Jethro came back from the ice-cream kiosk. What he didn't know was that Jethro had spotted some girls he knew and was chatting to them. Sam looked at the boys and at the same time noticed a small dinghy also beyond the ropes. As soon as Jethro got back he would have to see to them.

Thomas and Chris were getting hungry and decided to wander back to their picnic. Mum had packed all of Thomas's favourite food – peanut butter and jam sandwiches, crisps, cold sausages, lemonade – and some ham sandwiches and chicken legs for everybody else.

"Where's Rachel?" asked Mum.

"She's still swimming. She said she wasn't hungry," lied Thomas, who didn't want to wait for Rachel to get back. As it was his birthday Mum said they could tuck in; Rachel could have hers later.

Eventually Jethro got back to the lifeguard station with a half-melted ice lolly for Sam. But before Sam could eat it they heard a lot of angry voices further along the beach. It sounded as if there was a fight going on and both Jethro and Sam dashed down to sort out the trouble. Two families were squabbling over a stretch of sand. One couple were relaxing quietly and the other family were kicking a ball about. It kept landing on top of the first couple so they had grabbed the ball and refused to give it back. Only when Sam threatened both families with eviction from the beach did the situation calm down – the ball was returned and the footballers went further along the beach.

When Sam got back on station he noticed that the boys on the other side of the ropes were coming out of the sea and the dinghy seemed to have disappeared – he assumed it had gone back into the swimming area.

It was the first time that day Rachel had felt happy. She sat back in the dinghy and closed her eyes, with the lovely warm sun drying her after the splashing she'd had from the boys. Then she shivered as a gust of air cooled her down. She looked up and was amazed to see how far away she was from the swimming area. She tried to paddle back towards the shore but her arms became heavy and she flopped with exhaustion. It was a losing battle as the wind, tide and current pushed her further out to sea. No one seemed to notice her feeble shouts. Soon she was no longer in sight of the beach as the dinghy rounded a point and carried her further out to sea.

Rachel felt cold, very frightened and totally helpless. The sea looked dark and menacing, as if it was trying to drag her to some kind of doom. Where were her parents? Had nobody noticed where she was?

"Leave some food for Rachel," said Mum, as Thomas and Chris continued to stuff themselves.

Dad was lying back, relaxing in the sun. Mum looked down towards the swimming area and saw a number of yellow dinghies on the water. Rachel was probably on one of them, enjoying herself at last.

After sorting out the feud over the football, Sam and Jethro relaxed at their lookout shelter. Other than a few dinghies there weren't many swimmers in the water because it was lunchtime. The girls who knew Jethro came by and they sat around chatting.

The tide was going out. Gary hadn't caught anything and he was hungry. He decided to call it a day. He had set up his fishing rod on a rock just beyond the sandy bay. As he started to pack his things away he noticed a yellow dingy floating by – it seemed to be drifting out to sea. A girl was waving frantically but then she stopped as she rounded the point. Gary realised immediately she was in trouble and, dropping his fishing-tackle box, reached for his mobile phone. But he couldn't get a signal. He was obviously too low down – he would have to climb up the path and get to the top of the cliff.

Gary left his fishing gear where it was and started to run up the path. As he got higher he kept trying his phone. At last, just near the top, his 999 call was finally made!

Rachel was in despair – surely somebody had seen her float out to sea! She had tried paddling again but she was too cold and she'd lost the feeling in her hands and arms. She sat back, crying, and put her hands under her armpits to try to get them warm again. Then she heard the motor! She looked wildly around and saw the most wonderful sight – the orange lifeboat racing towards her! Somebody had seen her!

Discussion:

1. What do you think Rachel's parents' reaction will be when she turns up in a lifeboat?
2. What will her parents say to the two lifeguards?
3. Why was there an area marked off for swimming?
4. How much was Rachel to blame for the predicament she found herself in? What would have happened if Gary hadn't seen her?
5. What kind of safety precautions should her parents have taken?

14
It's Only One Cigarette

THEME: the risks associated with smoking

*A*s she inhaled the smoke she could feel a burning sensation as it travelled down the back of her throat and into her lungs. She began to cough uncontrollably, hardly able to catch her breath.

"*I thought it was your first!*" said Janine. "*Keep puffing at it – you'll soon get used to it.*"

How do we know a girl is smoking for the first time? Why do you think she's doing it?

Here is the whole story.

"Why does he send you money like that?" asked Yasmin.

"You know you get Mother's Day and Father's Day, well my Uncle Dave says it's Niece's Day and sends me money," explained Julie.

"I wish I had an uncle like that, sending me twenty quid for no reason at all!" exclaimed Rachel. The three friends were sitting in the park by the swings, where they often met after school.

"He's always been like that," said Julie. "He and Auntie Liz can't have children so they give presents to their nieces and nephews."

"What are you going to do with the money?" asked Yasmin.

"I thought I might go into town this weekend and buy some CDs."

"We'll come as well and help you, won't we, Yas?" suggested Rachel.

Just then two older girls, Janine and Claire, wandered into the park, saw the three friends and sat down on the grass next to them.

"Watcha, girls!" greeted Janine in her usual way. She reached into her pocket and pulled out a packet of cigarettes. She handed one to Claire and lit them with a cheap lighter. She tossed the lighter into the air, caught it and then put it back in her pocket. Both girls leaned back against a tree and drew heavily on the cigarettes.

"That's better," sighed Janine. "I've been dying for a fag all day."

"Do you girls want one?" asked Claire.

"Hey, don't go giving me fags away! I've only got one left," said Janine.

"Maybe someone might lend us some money then we can buy a new packet and share them around," suggested Claire, looking hard at the three girls.

"Julie's the only one with money," said Yasmin. Julie glared angrily at her for mentioning the money.

"Come on, lend us three quid. We'll give it back to you tomorrow."

Julie wanted to say no, but her friends weren't supporting her so she reached into her bag and took out the new £20 note her Uncle Dave had sent.

"Ta! I won't be a minute," said Claire, snatching the money and heading off to the park entrance. There was a newsagent just across the road. She wasn't gone long and when she returned she had a new packet of cigarettes. She gave the change back to Julie.

"There's only ten pounds here!" cried Julie.

"They were more expensive than I thought," replied Claire, winking at Janine.

She opened the packet and offered the girls a cigarette. Julie was surprised when Rachel and Yasmin both accepted immediately. She knew they had tried it before but both said they didn't like it. When the packet was in front of her she reached out and took a cigarette. It's only one cigarette, she thought, it won't hurt you.

Julie watched the others as their cigarettes were lit. She watched how they sucked the smoke into their mouths and blew it out. She saw how they coyly giggled and held their cigarette between their fingers, trying to act really cool.

"Have you smoked before?" Janine had seen how Julie looked at the others and how worried she seemed.

Julie nodded her head. "Of course I have!" She could feel the heat from the flame of the lighter as Claire lit her cigarette. She copied the others and sucked deeply. As she inhaled the smoke she could feel a burning sensation as it travelled down the back of her throat and into her lungs. She began to cough uncontrollably, hardly able to catch her breath.

"I thought it was your first!" said Janine. "Keep puffing at it – you'll soon get used to it."

Julie felt embarrassed and she wanted to run away but pride stopped her. She took more puffs, but this time she kept the smoke in her mouth and didn't inhale it into her lungs. As she smoked her cigarette she began to get used to it and to know how much to breathe in without coughing. She was actually disappointed when she finished it.

"Did you enjoy it?" asked Janine.

"Yeh, it was OK." Julie felt pleased with herself. Smoking was really easy. What was all the fuss about smoking being dangerous? She felt fine.

"Here, seeing as how you paid for them, take another one," said Janine, offering the pack to Julie. She took a cigarette, but as much as she'd enjoyed the first one she didn't have time to smoke it there and then. She put it into her pocket, stood up and said goodbye to the others.

"I'm home!" shouted Julie as she came through the front door. She threw her school bag under the stairs and wandered into the kitchen. She wanted a drink of water because she still had the taste of the cigarette in her mouth and it wasn't very nice. When she went through the kitchen door she saw her mother sitting at the table, crying.

Julie rushed over to her mother. "Mum, what's wrong?"
At first her mother couldn't say anything; seeing Julie made her cry even more. After a few minutes she was able to compose herself.

"It's your Uncle Dave. Aunt Liz just phoned to say that he's got lung cancer."

"I don't understand. How did he get that?" asked a bewildered Julie.

"It's from the cigarette smoke. They think he's only got a few months to live!" cried her mother.

"But, Mum, I've never seen Uncle Dave smoke."

"You know he works in a pub? Well, he's been breathing in other people's smoke for over twenty years. It's not just smokers who can get lung cancer; the smoke can be dangerous to others as well."

Julie put her hand into her pocket and gripped the cigarette. She rushed out of the kitchen, up the stairs and into her bedroom. She pulled the cigarette out and stared at it. It seemed so small and harmless, and yet it was a killer. She went into the bathroom, threw the cigarette down the toilet and watched it flush away.

Discussion:
1. Why didn't Julie refuse the cigarette?
2. What are the effects of smoking?

(Include reference to lung cancer, chest complaints, bad breath, smelly clothes, stained teeth, fire hazard, etc.)

3. Roy Castle was a famous entertainer who never smoked but died of lung cancer because of the smoke he inhaled when he worked in clubs. This is called passive smoking. What other people are likely to suffer from this?

15
Ten Green Bottles

THEME: alcohol abuse and its effects

He felt brave; he felt he could do anything. He jumped on to the wall, arms out to help him balance. He stood grinning at the others and they all shouted, "One leg, one leg, one leg!"

He slowly raised his leg as high as it would go, but then his head started spinning. He lost his balance and fell backwards on to the shattered glass below.

What would make someone feel they could do anything, even if it was very dangerous?

Here is the whole story.

It was a cold night but some of the older boys had started a small fire from old broken pallets. Mark, Tom and Leroy approached the group huddled around the blaze. They were in the parking bay of a derelict factory, hidden from the view of any prying eyes. There was a security fence around the building but the owner had long ago given up trying to keep people out, especially as the buildings were soon to be knocked down to make way for a new factory.

One of the older boys had managed to get a couple of cases of bottled beer and was selling them at £2 a bottle He seemed to be doing quite a good trade as there were several empties already and a pervading smell of beer in the air. Mark had talked Tom and Leroy into going along. He had heard about these drinking dens and wanted to see what it was all about.

"We've got three new recruits," said Robbie, the one who was selling beer. "You can only join us if you're buying."

"No problem," replied Mark as he took two pound coins out of his pocket. Tom and Leroy held back, they both knew they would be in trouble with their parents if they were caught drinking.

"You as well," said Robbie, looking threatenly at them.

"Can we share a bottle?" asked Tom. "We only brought one pound each."

"What do you think, lads? Should they share a bottle?" Robbie shouted to the other boys around the fire. They didn't care, so Tom and Leroy got away with having a bottle between them.

For Tom and Leroy this was the first time they had drunk beer without being supervised by a parent. Sipping your dad's beer is one thing, but having your own is quite something else. At first they were tentative about taking a swig out of the bottle but they soon lost their inhibitions and were enjoying the freedom. Mark had been to one of Robbie's drinking dens before and had sometimes drunk himself to the point of being quite sick. This didn't put him off, though, and he enjoyed the challenge of keeping up with the older boys.

"Ten green bottles!" the older boys began to shout. This was a game they played once they had ten empty bottles. There was a short wall, about a metre high, along the parking bay of the factory. They placed the ten green beer bottles along the wall and began singing, "There were ten green bottles sitting on the wall. If one green bottle should accidentally fall ..." The boys threw stones at a bottle until it smashed. "... there'll be nine green bottles sitting on the wall." This continued until all the bottles had been either knocked off the wall or smashed.

By now all the boys were getting very loud and were staggering about from the effects of the beer. Tom and Leroy had drunk a lot less but even the half bottle they'd had each was making them rather giggly. At one point Leroy grabbed the bottle from Tom as he was drinking and Tom spilled beer all over his jacket. He didn't realise at the time what the consequence of that would be!

"Time for the initiation!" shouted Robbie. The other boys started shouting, "Mark, Mark, Mark!"

Mark walked over to Robbie who led him to the wall. "Now that you've been here three times you must have the initiation! This is your task: you've got to stand on the wall for five minutes and do anything we say without falling off."

Mark looked at the wall – this was easy, he thought. He felt brave; he felt he could do anything. He jumped on to the wall, arms out to help him balance. He stood grinning at the others and they all shouted, "One leg, one leg, one leg!"

He slowly raised his leg as high as it would go but then his head started spinning. He lost his balance and fell backwards on to the shattered glass below. Shards of broken beer bottles pierced his legs, arms and back. Though his mind was befuddled with the alcohol, he could still feel great pain all over his body and he screamed.

Tom and Leroy ran to the wall and peered over. It was dark but they could see Mark lying on the ground, crying out with pain. They turned round to Robbie and the other boys but they just laughed. "He's failed the initiation!" shouted Robbie. He picked up the last few bottles and he and his friends wandered away.

Tom climbed over the wall and helped Mark to stand up. "Leroy, help me get him over the wall," urged Tom.

The two boys gently eased Mark back to the other side of the wall. Then they walked out of the factory yard and into the street. They stood under a street-light and inspected Mark's wounds. The glass hadn't pierced his jacket but there was blood dripping down the back of his legs and all over his hands.

"What shall we do?" asked Leroy anxiously.

"You live nearest – we'll have to take him to your house," suggested Tom.

"No way! My parents will know what we've been doing!"

"Owww, it really hurts!" wailed Mark.

"OK," said Leroy, realising that he didn't have much choice.

Leroy lived about ten minutes away, walking quickly, but it took them double that time to get Mark there. "Mum! Mum!" Leroy shouted when they entered the house. "Come quick! Mark has hurt himself!"

"My goodness me! What have you boys been up to?"

"Nothing, Mum. Mark fell over in the road. He fell in some broken glass. It was an accident."

"Oh yes, and where did you get the beer?"

"We haven't been drinking any beer."

"Leroy, don't you dare lie to me! You boys smell like a brewery. Look, Tom has it all over his jacket! Come into the kitchen and let's see what we can do."

Leroy's mother helped Mark into the kitchen where she lay him face down on the kitchen table. Some of the glass had fallen out during the walk home but there were a couple of big pieces still embedded in his legs. It was decided that calling an ambulance would be the quickest way for Mark to get to the hospital. Mark's parents were telephoned and they decided to go straight to the hospital. Leroy's mother also called Tom's parents, who came over to pick him up. He had some explaining to do, especially as his clothes smelt as though they'd been washed in beer!

Discussion:

1. What effects does alcohol have on the body?

(Discuss the various effects and mention that this is accentuated in young children because of their low body mass, meaning that a small amount of alcohol will have a greater effect on them.)

2. Why did the boys who met round the back of the factory want to be hidden from view?

(Talk about the fact that they were breaking the law. The older boys who supplied the alcohol could be in real trouble.)

3. Why did the boys take these kinds of risks?